Culpeper County, Virginia

Deed Book Abstracts

1778–1779

Ruth and Sam Sparacio

HERITAGE BOOKS
2022

HERITAGE BOOKS
AN IMPRINT OF HERITAGE BOOKS, INC.

Books, CDs, and more—Worldwide

For our listing of thousands of titles see our website
at
www.HeritageBooks.com

Published 2022 by
HERITAGE BOOKS, INC.
Publishing Division
5810 Ruatan Street
Berwyn Heights, Md. 20740

International Standard Book Number
Paperbound: 978-1-68034-501-8

pp.   On margin: D D to WM. THOMPSON Septr 7th 1779

1-   THIS INDENTURE TRIPARTITE made 11 February 1777 Between BERNARD MOORE

3-   Esqr. only Acting Executor of the Last Will and Testament of JOHN SPOTSWOOD
Esquire Deceased of the first part and ALEXANDER SPOTSWOOD Eldest Son and Heir
at Law of said John of the Second part and WILLIAM THOMPSON of County of Culpeper of
the third part. Whereas MAJOR GENERAL ALEXANDER SPOTSWOOD formerly of the
County of ORANGE being seized of land and by his Last Will and Testament did give all
his land to his Son John Spotswood but power to charge any of said lands (the Mine
Tract Excepted) with fortunes for his Daughters said John Spotswood died leaving issue
Alexander Spotswood Party hereto his Eldest Son and heir at Law and Two Daughters
ANN and MARY said John before his death made his Last Will and Testament and
charged the lands in Counties of Orange and Culpeper with payment of fortunes to his
said Daughters and fortunes are become payable said Alexander hath exposed to sale
part of the land in the Counties of Orange and Culpeper and among others William
Thompson hath become a purchaser of a Tract of land in the County of Culpeper containing Two hundred and sixty acres bounded Begining at a white oak corner to JAMESS
lott thence South to a Branch down the branch to a poplar stump just before the
CHURCH ROAD thence North to a red oak corner to BRANHAMs lott thence South to two
red oak saplins in MARSHALLs line thence North with Marshalls line to a red oak Corner in said Thompsons line thence to YOUNGs lines thence with his line to three maples
in BUCKRUN Corner to EDWARD WATKINS thence with his line to the Begining NOW
THIS INDENTURE WITNESSETH that for sum of One hundred and thirty two pounds Eight
paid to Alexander Spotswood the Younger and by him applyed towards the payments of
his Sisters fortunes said Alexander Spotswood together with Bernard Moore have sold
unto the said William Thompson the aforesaid two hundred and sixty acres of land . . . . .

In presence of EDWARD VOSS,   Alexander Spotswood

     AARON LANE, ROBT. COLEMAN JR.

At a Court held for Culpeper County the 18th of August 1777
This Indenture was partly proved by the Oaths of Aaron Lane and Robert Coleman jr.
and ordered to be Certified and at a Court held 17 August 1778 was fully proved by the
Oath of Edward Voss and ordered to be recorded.

pp.   On margin: D. D. to WILLIAM S. THOMPSON Septr 7 1779

3-   THIS INDENTURE TRIPARTITE made the 11th of February 1777 Between BERNARD

6   MOORE Esqr. only Acting Executor of JOHN SPOTSWOOD Esquire Deceased of the
first part, ALEXANDER SPOTSWOOD Eldest Son and Heir at Law of the said John of
the Second part, and WILLIAM THOMPSON of the third part. Whereas MAJOR GENERAL
ALEXANDER SPOTSWOOD formerly of the County of ORANGE by his Last Will and Testament devised all his land to his son John Spotswood with power to sell said lands (his
Mine Run Tract excepted) with such fortunes for his Daughters and the said John died
leaving two Daughters said John in his Will charged the lands in the Counties of Orange
and Culpeper with payment of fortunes of his Daughters the said Alexander has exposed
to sale the said lands and among others William Thompson hath become purchaser of
two parcels in the County of Culpeper one containing Two hundred and thirty acres and
the other One hundred and sixty three acres bounded Begining at two white oaks
standing on the SCHOOL HOUSE PATH near ROBERT JOHNSTONs fence runing thence

South to two white oaks on South side of MR. LIGHTFOOTs ROAD thence North to a white oak on a branch side near said Thompsons fence East to two red oaks standing on the East side of the COURTHOUSE ROAD and on the South side of a branch thence South to the Begining; the other begining as followeth one red oak standing on a point near a branch Corner to WILLIAM NASHs Lott thence with his line North to the MAIN ROAD known by the name of BLOODWORTHs thence up said Road North to three red oaks Corner to the Lott surveyed to JNO. ROWSONs Lott thence North to the Begining NOW THIS INDENTURE WITNESSETH that pursuant to the Wills of Alexander Spotswood the Elder and John Spotswood and for sum of Three hundred and ninety three pounds Currency paid by William Thompson to said Alexander Spotswood the Younger and applyed towards payment of his Sisters fortunes the said Alexander Spotswood together with Bernard Moore hath granted unto William Thompson Three hundred and ninety three acres of land . . . .

In presence of EDWARD VOSS,   Alexander Spotswood
          AARON LANE, ROBT. COLEMAN JR.
  At a Court held for Culpeper County the 18th of August 1777
This Indenture partly proved by the Oaths of Aaron Lane and Robert Coleman jr two of the witnesses thereto & ordered to be certified and at a Court held for the said County the 17th of August 1778 was fully proved by the Oath of Edward Voss and ordered to be recorded.

pp.   THIS INDENTURE made the 9th August 1778 Between JOHN BERRY SENR. and
6-   JEMIMA his of County of Culpeper Parish of Bromfield of one part and ROBERT
10   MILLAR of same County and Parish Witnesseth that said John Berry and Jemima
          his Wife for the sum Seventy five pounds Current money of Virginia have
granted unto the said Robert Millar and his heirs One hundred and forty acres of land in Culpeper County and Bromfield Parish on the waters of the Beaverdam Run bounded Begining at three chesnut oaks on the north branch of the Beaverdam Run and runing thence North to three chesnut oaks on the North side of the north branch of the Hazel River on the side of the BEAVERDAM MOUNTAIN thence North to four chesnut oaks on the North side of the NORTH MOUNTAIN near THORNTONS PASS thence South crossing the Beaver Dam Run to a Chesnut Oak on the South side of Beaverdam Run thence South to the Begining . . . .

In presence of BENJAMIN LILLARD,   John Berry
          WILLIAM JONES, GEORGE PASSONS,   Jemima Berry
          JOHN SLAUGHTER, GEO. WETHERALL
  The Commonwealth of Virginia to JOHN SLAUGHTER and GEO. WETHERALL and BEN ROBERTS Gent Whereas John Berry Senr. and Jemima his Wife have sold land in County of Culpeper unto Robert Millar and Whereas the said Jemima cannot cannot travel to our County Court of Culpeper to make acknowledgement of the said conveyance we give you power to go to the said Jemima and receive her acknowledgement whether she doth the same freely and when you have examined her as aforesaid that you Certifie us thereof in our County Court. Witness JOHN JAMESON Clerk of our said Court this 17th of August 1778.
  By Virtue of the within Commission we did personally go to the said Jemima and examined her apart from her husband touching her acknowledgement and she freely acknowledged the same. Given under our hands this 9th of Septr. 1778.
                              JOHN SLAUGHTER   GEO. WETHERALL;
  At a Court held for Culpeper County the 21st day of Septr 1778
This Indenture with the Commission & Certificate is ordered to be recorded.

pp.   THIS INDENTURE made this 14th of March 1776 Between ISAAC CAMPBELL of the
10-   County of Culpeper of one part and THOMAS PRATT of the County of Culpeper
12   Witnesseth that for the sum Fifty pounds current money of Virginia to the said
        Isaac Campbell paid the said Isaac Campbell and MARY ELING hath granted said
Thomas Pratt his heirs two hundred and forty two acres of land bounded Begining at a
pine Corner to THOMAS PRATT thence North to a pine and R O in said CHRISTIAN RINERs
line thence South to a poplar and Ring: 0 in a branch Corner to Riner and REDMAN
thence South to a white oak on a branch Corner to CROSSWIT thence South to the
Begining . . . .
In presence of ABSOLOM BOBO,   Isaac Campbell
        STEPHEN HAYNES, GEORGE HUME
   At a Court held for Culpeper County the 17th of August 1778
This Indenture ordered to be recorded.

pp.   On margin: D D JS. BROWNING SEN 1795
13-   THIS INDENTURE made the third day of March 1778 Between JAMES HICKMAN of
14   County of Culpeper of one part and SUSANNA BROWNING Daughter of the said
        James Hickman of the same County of other part Witnesseth that said James
Hickman for love he hath for his said Daughter doth give unto the said Susanna
Browning Wife of JAMES BROWNING all that land whereon James Browning now liveth
in the County aforesaid containing one hundred and seventy eight acres of land
bounded Begining at three chesnuts on the side of a Mountain thence South to a red oak
Corner to THOMAS McCLANAHAN thence North to a red oak Cornering in DAVID HICK-
MANs line thence North to a chesnut in THORNTONs line thence with Thorntons line to
the begining containing one hundred and seventy eight acres of land it being part of a
tract of land formerly granted to ROBERT CAVE which said land the said James Hickman
doth by these presents grant unto Susanna Browning . . . .
In presence of ROBT. EASTHAM JR.,   James Hickman
        JASON ISBELL, EDWIN HICKMAN,
        GEORGE CALVERT JUNR.
        P. EASTHAM, GEORGE EASTHAM
   At a Court held for Culpeper County the 17th of August 1778
This Indented Deed of Gift ordered to be recorded.

pp.   THIS INDENTURE made the XXI day of September 1778 Between STEPHEN FISHER
14-   and MAGDALENE his Wife of County Culpeper and Parish of Bromfield of one
16   part and JASPER STARR of the same County and Parish Witnesseth that Stephen
        Fisher and Magdalene his Wife hath granted unto said Jasper Starr land in the
aforesaid County and Parish it being the land whereon the said Jasper Starr now lives,
for Five hundred pounds Current money of Virginia, which said land is bounded
Begining at two white oaks on the South side of the Robinson River thence South
leaving the Branch a red oak on aride near an OLD ROAD thence North to the mouth of
Quaker Run thence down the said Run and River to the Begining containing two hundred acres of land . . . .

                                                            Stephen Fisher
   At a Court held for Culpeper County the 17th August 1778   Magdalene Fisher
This Indenture ordered to be recorded previous to which the
said Magdalene was first examined as the Law directs.

pp.   THIS INDENTURE made the 17th September 1778 Between JOHN ALFRED HEAD and
16-   ELIZABETH his Wife of County of Culpeper of one part and HADLEY HEAD of

18   ORANGE COUNTY Witnesseth that said John Alfred Head and Elizabeth his Wife
         for the sum Fifteen pounds current money of Virginia hath granted unto the
said Hadley Head his heirs forever land in the Parish of Bromfield County of Culpeper
containing Eighty eight acres and bounded Begining at three black oaks Corner to JOHN
BEAL thence with his line South to a Corner claimed by the said BOBO thence South to
two pines Corner to AMBROSE BARNETT thence North to three pines on the North side
the head of a branch one of which is marked I × T formerly a Corner to GIBBENs now
LYNEs thence North to three pines on the North side of MEDLEYS ROAD Corner to a line
beloning to JOHN MEDLEYs Orphans thence South to the Begining . . . .
Presence of CHS. CARTER,   John Alfred Head
         BENJAMIN FENNILL
    At a Court held for Culpeper County the 17th of August 1778
This Indenture ordered to be recorded previous to which the said Elizabeth was privily
examined as the Law directs.

pp.   THIS INDENTURE made the 21st of September 1778 Between WILLIAM EDGMAN
18-   and ELISABETH his Wife of County of Culpeper of one part land JAMES PANNILL
20   of County aforesaid Witnesseth that the said William Edgman and Elisabeth his
         Wife for sum of One hundred and seventy five pounds current money of Vir-
ginia have sold unto the said James Pannill his heirs 182 acres in Culpeper County and
Bromfield Parish in the Little Fork of Rappanock in the fork of the Rush River and the
same being part of Four hundred acres granted to HENRY TYLER by the right honourable THOMAS LORD FAIRFAX Proprietor of the Northern Neck of Virginia by Deed from
the Proprietors Office the 18th of February 1748 and by the said Tyler sold to JOHN
YANCEY, and by the said Yancey was sold to JOHN MURPHIN and by the said Murphin
was sold to the said William Edgman and the 180 acres bounded Begining at a Spanish
Oak standing on the bank of the North Fork of the Rush River and runs thence South to
a Gum on the bank of the South Fork of the Rush River in PHILIP JACOB IRIONs line
thence with his line North to a Hikory markt H×T on a Stony ridge thence North to a
Spanish Oak in a large vale near the foot of the BLUE RIDGE thence South to a hikory &
maple markt 9 H on the Rush River Bank thence down the courses to the begining
place To have and to hold the said Tract of one hundred and eighty two acres of land . . .
In presence of JAMES GAINES,   William Edgman
         WM. WRIGHT   Elisabeth × Edgman
    At a Court held for Culpeper County the 17th of August 1778
This Indenture Together with the Receipt endorsed ordered to be recorded, Previous to
which the said Elisabeth was first privily Examined as the Law directs.

pp.   On margin: D D Self 1789
20-   THIS INDENTURE made the 21st of September 1778 Between WILLIAM EDGMAN
23   and ELISABETH his Wife of County of Culpeper of one part and WILLIAM WRIGHT
         of County aforesaid Witnesseth that William Edgman and Elisabeth his Wife for
the sum of Ninety five pounds current money of Virginia have sold unto the said William Wright his heirs Ninety eight acres of land in Culpeper County and Bromfield
Parish in the Little Fork of Rappahannock River in the fork of the Rush River the same
being part of four hundred acres granted to HENRY TYLER by the right Honourable
THOMAS LORD FAIRFAX Proprietor of the Northern Neck of Virginia by Deed from the
Proprietors Office dated the 18th of February 1748 and by the said Henry Tyler sold to
JOHN YANCEY and by said John Yancey was sold unto JOHN MURPHIN and by said Murphin was sold unto William Edgman and said Ninety eight acres is bounded Begining at
a Spanish Oak in the bank of the North Fork of the Rush River on the South side thereof

Corner to JAMES PENNILL and runs thence South to a Gum on the North side of the South Fork of the Rush River in PHIL. JACOB IRONs line thence with his line South to two white oaks Corner to Tylers deed thence North to two white oaks on the North side of the North Fork of the Rush River to the begining place . . . .

Presence of JAMES GAINES,   William Edgman
        JAMES PENNILL   Elisabeth ✗ Edgman
    At a Court held for Culpeper County the 17th of August 1778
This Indenture ordered to be recorded Previous to which the said Elisabeth was first privily examined according to Law.

p.   I JEREMIAH DEER of the County of Culpeper I do hereby give to MORDECAI
23   BOUGHAN one Bay mare black main and Tail and saddle branded on the near
        buttock I P about four feet seven 9 or eight inches high Star in her fore-
head snip on her nose I do hereby Warrant the said Mare aginst all persons whatso-
ever. Witness my hand this 5th day of April 1778.
                                                            Jeremiah ✗ Deer
        VINCENT BOUGHAN,
        AMBROSE BROWN, JOHN ONEIL
    At a Court held for Culpeper County the 17th of August 1778
This Indented Deed of Gift ordered to be recorded.

pp.   THIS INDENTURE made the 15th of August 1778 Between ADAM YEAGER of the
23-   County of Culpeper of one part and ADAM YEAGER JUNIOR of County aforesaid
25   Witnesseth that said Adam Yeager for good causes but more for Love he doth
        bear unto his Son and for five shillings doth give unto said Adam Yeager Junr.
his heirs forever One hundred and twenty three acres of land being part of a Tract he
bought of JOHN NELSON in said County of Culpeper and Parish of Bromfield on the
branches of the Robinson River and bounded Begining at two small white oaks thence
South thence to the Begining . . . .

In presence of WM. C. BROWN,   Adam A Yeager
    JAMES BARBOUR, MOSES BROYLES
    At a Court held for Culpeper County the 17th of August 1778
This Indented Deed of Gift ordered to be recorded.

pp.   On margin: D. D. to WM. BRADLEY 1785
25-   THIS INDENTURE made the Twenty Second day of August 1777 Between GEORGE
28   THORNTON and MARY his Wife of the County of SPOTSYLVANIA of one part and
        THOMAS HALL of County of Culpeper Witnesseth that George Thornton and Mary
his Wife for sum One hundred pounds Virginia money have granted unto the said Thomas Hall his heirs land in County of Culpeper & Bromfield Parish between the Hazel
River and Hughs.s Rivers containing Two hundred acres land is bounded Begining at a
white oak on Hughes River thence North to two white oaks on the South side of the
MAIN ROAD thence up the said Road South thence West to a red oak on a Knowl thence
South to a Spanish Oak on a stony Knowl near said River formerly a Corner to DUFF and
STONEHOUSE thence down the diferent courses of the said river to the Begining . . . .

Presence of JOHN STROTHER,   Geo. Thornton
        JOHN SLAUGHTER, WILLIAM CHAMPE,   Mary Thornton
        JOHN THORNTON
    The Commonwealth of Virginia to JOHN STROTHER and JOHN SLAUGHTER Gent Whereas
George Thornton and Mary his Wife have sold land in the County of Culpeper unto Thomas Hall and Whereas the said Mary cannot travel to our said County Court to make acknowledgement of the said Conveyance we do give unto you power to personally go to

the said Mary and examine her apart from her husband whether she doth the same
freely and when you have received her acknowledgement that you Certifie us thereof
in our County Court. Witness JOHN JAMESON Clk of our said Court at the Courthouse the
22nd of August 1778 and the third year of the Commonwealth.
  Culpeper SCT In Obedience to the within Commission we did go to the said Mary Thornton and she did freely acknowledge the same. Given this 22nd day August 1778.
                             JOHN STROTHER   JOHN SLAUGHTER
  At a Court held for Culpeper County the 17th of August 1778
This Indenture with the Commission & Certificate is ordered to be recorded.

pp.   On margin: D D to NEATHER Augt 21 1780
28-   THIS INDENTURE made the 19th of October 1778 Between JOHN STROTHER and
30   MARY his Wife of Culpeper County of one part and GODFREY NEATHER of the
         same County Witnesseth that John Strother and Mary his Wife for the sum
Twenty five Pounds Virginia money have granted unto said Godfrey Neather Fifty one
acres of land being part of a tract of land granted unto SAMUEL KENNERLY containing
four hundred acres by the Right Honourable THOMAS LORD FAIRFAX dated June 1748
and recorded in the Proprietors Office Book G Folio (66) and is bounded begining at a
white oak in COVINTONs line thence North to a large white oak on the South side of a
branch thence up the said Branch North East to a Double white oak Corner to DUNAWAY
thence South to the begining . . . .

                                                                        John Strother
  At a Court held for Culpeper County the 19th of Octr 1778   Mary Strother
This Indenture ordered to be recorded.

pp.   On margin: D D W. WALKER 1791
30-   THIS INDENTURE made this eighth day of June 1778 Between WILLIAM ROEBUCK
32   and MARY his Wife of one part and WILLIAM ZACHARY Witnesseth that said
         William Roebuck and Mary his Wife for sum Two hundred and Forty pounds cur-
rent money hath granted unto said William Zachary his heirs forever one hundred and
forty acres of land in the County of Culpeper bounded begining at a pine in CAVES
ROAD thence North to one post oak on a branch thence North to a Double pine near
SMITHs Run thence up the several courses of the said Run to the mouth of BURFORDs
Spring Branch thence to the begining . . . .
In presence of JOHN GIBBS,   William Roebuck
         ZACHARIAS GIBBS, JOSHUA LINDSAY,   Mary Roebuck
         JOHN FAULKNER
  At a Court held for Culpeper County the 19th of October 1778
This Indenture ordered to be recorded Previous to which the said Mary was first privily
examined according to Law.

pp.   THIS INDENTURE made the 22nd of September 1778 Between HENRY FIELD and
32-   his Wife JENNY FIELD of the County of Culpeper of one part & JOSEPH SANDFORD
34   of the County of WESTMORELAND Witnesseth that for Sum Two hundred and Sixty
         pounds current money of Virginia the said Henry Field & his Wife have sold
unto the said Joseph Sandford one hundred and thirty acres of land in the aforesaid
County and bounded begining at two thorn Bushes standing on the Bank of Mountain
Run thence South to a Pecimon Bush on the Bank of Mountain Run by the mouth of a
gully thence South to a hikory saplin in an Island of Thorny Branch thence North to
two white oaks by a PATH thence South to three white oaks by a small PATH thence
North to two white oaks between GEORGE ROBERTS and the land of Mr. JACKSONs thence

with said line North to the Begining on Mountain Run . . . .
Presence D. GREENWOOD,   Henry Field
        GEORGE ROBERTS, JOHN JETT,
        LEONARD BARNES
  At a Court held for Culpeper County the 19th of October 1778
This Indenture ordered to be recorded.

pp   On margin: D D FRAS. MADDISON Octr 3d. 1780
34-   THIS INDENTURE TRIPARTITE made the 28th of November 1777 Between BENJA-
39   MIN GRYMES of County of ORANGE and SALLEY his Wife of the first part and
         CHARLES GRYMES of the TOWN and COUNTY of YORK of the second part and
JAMES MADISON of County of Orange of the third part. Whereas the Honourable PHILIP
GRYMES Esquire being at the time of his death seized of Twelve thousand acres of land
in the County of Culpeper formerly Orange County by his Last Will and Testament did
devise the same to his two Sons the said Charles and Benjamin to be equally divided as
by said Will proved in the County Court of MIDDLESEX and Whereas Benjamin Grymes
hath for consideration hereafter mentioned sold to said James Madison Two thousand
three hundred and one acres of land bounded being part of the said Twelve thousand
acres to which sale the said Charles Grymes hath consented NOW THIS INDENTURE WIT-
NESSETH that the said Benjamin Grymes and Salley his Wife for the sum of One Thousand five hundred and Forty seven pounds Fourteen shillings current money to him
and said Charles Grymes for sum Five shillings current money to him have granted
unto the said James Madison his heirs forever the said Two thousand three hundred and
one acres of land situate in County of Culpeper bounded Begining at a white oak on the
Rappidan River a little above JACKS FORD and Corner to JAMES WALKER Gent. runing
thence North to a poplar on MEDLEYS ROAD thence North to a white oak on the North
side of the OAKEY RIDGE Corner to ROBERT ALCOCK thence South to four bushes on FRYS
ROAD another Corner to the said Alcock thence along the said Road near the head of a
valley and Corner to said Alcock thence South to a hikory on the Rappidan River at the
GERMAN FORD thence up the Meanders of the said River to the begining . . . .
Presence ALEXR. WAUGH,   Benjamin Grymes
        ROBT. ALCOCK, BEN. PORTER,   Salley Grymes
        NICHL. PORTER, JOHN TERRILL,   Ch. Grymes
        ROBT. TERRILL JR.
Sealed & Delivered by Ben. Grymes in Presence of
        ROWLAND THOMAS, WILLIAM WALKER, THOMAS BARBOUR,
        ROBT. ALCOCK, AMBROSE MADISON, JAMES WALKER
Culpeper Sct In the name of the Commonwealth of Virginia to Rowland Thomas and
CATLETT CONWAY and Thomas Barbour Gentlemen Whereas Benjamin Grymes Gent of
County of Orange and Salley his Wife have sold unto James Madison Gent of the County
of Orange Estate in the County of Culpeper and Whereas the said Salley cannot travel to
our said County Court of Culpeper to make acknowledgement of the said conveyance we
give you power to examine her privately and apart from her husband and whether she
doth the same frely and that you Certify us thereof in our County Court. Witness JOHN
JAMESON Clerk this 21st of September 1778.
  Orange to Wit By Virtue of the Commission we the Subscribers did on the 7th day of
October 1778 go to the said Salley Grymes and haveing examined her apart from her
husband do certify that she declared she freely acknowledged the conveyance in the
said Indenture.   ROWLAND THOMAS   THOS. BARBOUR
  At a Court held for Culpeper County the 19th of October 1778
This Indenture with a Commission thereto annexed and Certificate endorsed is ordered

to be recorded.

pp.   On margin: D. D. to Mr. THOS. LATHAM May 19th 1780
39-   THIS INDENTURE made the 19th day of October 1778 Between NATHANIEL PEN-
41   DLETON and BETTY his Wife of one part and THOMAS LATHAM of County of Cul-
         peper Witnesseth that the said Nathaniel Pendleton and Betty his Wife for sum
of Seven hundred pounds current money have granted unto the said Thomas Latham
his heirs forever land in the County of Culpeper and St. Marks Parish and on the South
side of Mountain Run being the land whereon the said Nathaniel Pendleton now lives
containing Two hundred and seventy six acres one half acres and is bounded Begining
at a white oak Corner to RICHARD POLLARD now JOHN CAMPs on a Branch thence North
to a red oak in CAPT. WATKINS now JOHN M. BELLs line Corner to JAMES HUNTER thence
with his line North with another of his lines to PHILIP CLAYTONs line thence with his
line to Mountain Run then up the said Run the several courses of the mouth of Hungry
Run to a BRIDGE at the Mouth of a Ditch thence up the said Ditch along the side of a
ROAD to Muddy Branch then up the Branch to the sd Pollard now Camps thence with
him up the said branch to the Fork thence up the South Fork to the begining . . . .

                                                          N. Pendleton
   At a Court held for Culpeper County the 19th of October 1778   Betty Pendleton
This Indenture ordered to be recorded Previous to which the
said Betty was first privily examined as the Law directs.

pp.   On margin: D D to JOHN WALKER 16th May 1780
41-   THIS INDENTURE made the Sixteenth day of December 1777 Between CHARLES
45   GRYMES of County of GLOUCESTER and BENJAMIN GRYMES and SALLY his Wife
         of County of ORANGE of one part and JAMES WALKER of County of Orange of
other part Witnesseth that Whereas the Honourable PHILIP GRYMES Esquire at the time
of his death was seized in about twelve thousand acres of land in the County of Culpeper
formerly Orange County by his Will did devise the same to his two Sons Charles and
Benjamin to be equally divided between them as by said Will recorded in the County
Court of MIDDLESEX and Whereas Charles and Benjamin Grymes hath for consideration
mentioned sold to the said James Walker One thousand three hundred and thirty acres
being part of the said Twelve thousand acres NOW THIS INDENTURE WITNESSETH that the
said Charles Grymes and Benjamin Grymes for the sum Three hudnred and forty eight
pounds Sixteen shillings current money to them paid do grant unto the said James
Walker his heirs One thousand three hundred and thirty acres of land in the County of
Culpeper which by a survey and plan made by JOSEPH WOOD Gent. is bounded Begining
at two small gums on the River bank Corner to Joseph Wood thence with Woods line
North to a white oak Corner to JOHN RODEHEIFER thence North to three pines in Rode-
heifers line South down MEDLEYS ROAD thence nearly with the said Road the following
courses (to wit) South-East-South-East to white oak saplins near JACKS FORD on the
river bank Corner to JAMES MADISON thence up the River to the Begining . . . .
Presence of BIRKETT DAVENPORT,   Chas. Grymes
         GEO. THORNTON, WM. MOORE,   Ben Grymes
         FRENCH STROTHER, MARTIN PICKETT   Sally Grymes
   Seald & Delivered by Ben Grymes in Presence of
         ROWLAND THOMAS, THOS. BARBOUR,. WM. WALKER,
         ROBT. ALCOCK, AMBS. MADISON
Culpeper Sct In name of the Commonwealth of Virginia to WILLIAM BELL, ROWLAND
THOMAS & THOS. BARBOUR Gent Whereas Charles Grymes of the County of Gloucester
and Benjamin Grymes and Salley his Wife of the County of Orange have conveyed land

in the County of Culpeper unto James Walker and Whereas the said Salley cannot travel to our County Court of Culpeper to make acknowledgement of the said Conveyance we do give unto you power to receive the acknowledgement which said Salley shall be willing to make before you and when you have received her said acknowledgement that you Certifie our Justices in our County Court thereof. Witness JOHN JAMESON Clerk of our said Court the 21st of September & in the year 1778.

Orange to Wit By Virtue of the Commission We the Subscribers did on the 7th day of October 1778 go to the said Salley Grymes and having examined her apart from her husband do Certifie that she freely acknowledged the conveyance. Witness our hands and seals the day & year above written.

ROWLAND THOMAS   THS. BARBOUR

At a Court held for Culpeper County the 19th day of October 1778
This Indenture with a Commission thereto annexed and Certificate endorsed is ordered to be recorded.

pp. 45-47 THIS INDENTURE made the 19th day of October 1778 Between JACOB COFER and MILDRED his Wife of County of ORANGE of one part and GEORGE EVE of the County of Culpeper Witnesseth that the said Jacob Cofer for sum of Fifty pounds current money hath sold unto the said George Eve in his actual possession ninety acres of land in the County of Culpeper and in the fork of Elk Run which said land the said Jacob Cofer and Mildred his Wife doth confirm unto the said George Eve bounded Begining at two white oaks by the OLD ROAD thence South to the Begining . . .

Presence of JAMES COFER,   Jacob + Cofer
       CHARLES COCKE, JOEL + COFER   Miley + Cofer

At a Court held for Culpeper County the 19th of Octr 1778
This Indenture ordered to be recorded Previous to which the said Milley was first privily examined according to Law.

pp. 48-49 On margin: D D 1794
THIS INDENTURE made this 19th day of October 1778 Between JACOB COFER of ORANGE COUNTY of one part and JOEL COFER of Culpeper County Witnesseth that said Jacob Cofer for the sum Seven shillings current money of Virginia hath granted unto Joel Cofer his heirs forever Ninety two acres of land in Culpeper County bounded Begining at the Division Corner to JAMES COFER at two red oaks Corner to GEORGE EVE thence South to three pines thence with James Cofers Division line to the begining furthermore Milley Wife to the said Jacob Cofer doth by these presents surrender up all her right of Dower unto said Joel Cofer forever . . . .

Presence GEORGE EVE,   Jacob + Cofer
       CHARLES COCK, JAMES COFER   Milley + Cofer

At a Court held for Culpeper County the 19th Octr 1778
This Indenture ordered to be recorded Previous to which the said Milley was first privily examined according to Law.

pp. 49-51 THIS INDENTURE made the 19th of October 1778 Between JACOB COFER of ORANGE COUNTY of one part and JAMES COFER of Culpeper County Witnesseth that the said Jacob Cofer for the sum Seven shillings current money of Virginia doth grant unto the said James Cofer his heirs forever One hundred and five acres of land in Culpeper County and bounded Begining at three pines thence North to OLD ROAD thence up the old Road South to GEORGE EVEs Corner thence East to Corner in Eves line North to the Begining To hold the same: Furthermore Milley the Wife of said Jacob Cofer doth by these presents surrender up all her right of Dower unto the said James

Cofer . . . .
Presence GEORGE EVE,   Jacob ✝ Cofer
     CHARLES COCK, JOEL ✝ COFER   Milley ⅄ Cofer
  At a Court held for Culpeper County the 19th October 1778
This Indenture Ordered to be recorded Previous to which the said Milley was first
privily examined according to Law.

pp.   THIS INDENTURE made the 19th of October 1778 Between JOHN SCOTT and HANNAH
51-   his Wife of County of Culpeper of one part and JOSHUA WILLIS of County aforesd
53   Witnesseth that said John Scott & Hanah his Wife for the sum Five hundred
      pounds Current money of Virginia do grant unto the said Joshua Willis his heirs
forever Three hundred acres of land in the County of Culpeper bounded Begining at a
hickory Corner to JOSEPH WOOD and runeth thence West to two red oaks on the West side
of a small branch thence down the branch South to a white oak saplin at the mouth of a
branch on the North side of JAMES BARBOURs MILL RUN thence up the said Run to two
red oak saplins in a line of a Pattent granted to JOHN DIXON deceased thence with the
said Dixons line North to two white oaks in a line between Joseph Wood and THOMAS
SCOTT thence with said line North to the begining . . . .

                                       John Scott
  At a Court held for Culpeper County the 19th Octr 1778   Hannah Scott
This Indenture ordered to be recorded; previous to which the
said Hannah was first privily examined according to Law.

pp.   On margin: D. D. to GEO. DOGGETT Jany 11th 1780
53-   THIS INDENTURE made the 15th of October 1778 Between ANDREW BOURN and
55   JANE his Wife of County of Culpeper of one part and GEORGE DOGGETT of same
      County Witnesseth that the said Andrew Bourn and Jane his Wife for the sum
One thousand pounds current money of the Commonwealth of Virginia have granted
unto the said George Doggett a parcel of land in the County aforesaid granted by Pattent
unto the said Andrew Bourn as will appear by Proprietors Office in Book G Folio (176)
and bearing date the 11th of June 1749 and bounded Begining at three pines Corner to
BUSHROD DOGGETT thence North West to one pine in the Point of the Fork a branch
thence East to one pine on the point of a hill thence N East to one white oak in JAMES
PENDLETONs line thence with his line South West to two white oaks Corner to said
Pendleton and Bushrod Doggett thence with said Doggetts line South to the begining
containing Five hundred and seventy five acres of land To Hold the said Tract unto
George Doggett and said Andrew Bourn and JEAN his Wife stand seised of right of In-
heritance in fee simple in granted land . . .

                                     Andrew Bourn
  At a Court held for Culpeper County the 19th Octr 1778   Jean ⅃ᵇ Bourn
This Indenture ordered to be recorded; Previous to which
the said Jean was first privily examined according to Law.

pp.   THIS INDENTURE made the 19th day of October 1778 Between HARRIS FREEMAN
56-   of County of Culpeper and ANN his Wife of one part and OBEDIAH WRIGHT of
58   County aforesaid Witnesseth that said Harris Freeman and Ann his Wife for the
      sum Eighty pounds current money of Virginia do grant unto the said Obediah
Wright one parcel of land bought by the said Freeman of EDWARD TURNER as by Deed
dated the thirty First 1777 will more fully appear and was purchased by Edward Turner
of JOHN McQUEEN and NATHANIEL BURDINE being in the County aforesaid on the Hedgman River near the GOHER MOUNTAIN containing One hundred and eighteen acres . . . .

Harris Freeman
Ann Freeman

The Commonwealth of Virginia to JAMES PENDLETON and JOHN WIGINTON Gentlemen Whereas Harris Freeman and Ann his Wife have sold unto Obediah Wright land in County of Culpeper and Whereas the said Ann cannot travel to our County Court of Culpeper to make acknowledgement of the said Conveyance we do give you power to personally go to the said Ann and examine her apart from her Husband and when you have received lher acknowledgment that you Certifie us thereof. Witness JOHN JAMESON Clerk of our said Court the 19th of October and in the Third Year of the Commonwealth.

Culpeper SCT In Obedience to the within Commission we caused the said Ann Freeman personally to come before us and examined her apart from her Husband touching her acknowledgement of the said conveyance when she freely acknowledged the same. Witness this 19th day of Octr. 1778.

                    JAMES PENDLETON   JOHN WIGGINTON

At a Court held for Culpeper County the 19th of Octr 1778 This Indentue with the Commission annexed and Certificate endorsed is ordered to be recorded.

pp.   THIS INDENTURE made the 18th of October 1778 Between THOMAS SLAUGHTER of
58-   County of FAIRFAX of one part and GEORGE WEATHERALL of County of Culpeper
60   Witnesseth that Thomas Slaughter for the sum One hundred and twenty pounds
           current money hath sold to him the said Geo. Wetherall his heirs land in the
County of Culpeper and on the Head of the Hazle River it being the tract of land said Thomas Slaughter formerly bought of FRANCIS KIRTLEY's Executors and is bounded Begining at four chesnut trees at the East side of a branch on the Hazle River thence South to one red oak on the Top of a Mountain South to three chesnuts on the side of a mountain on the falling ground of Hughs River thence North crossing a large Ivy Point and Branch of the Hazle River to the Begining containing One hundred and seventy four acres of land . . . .
Presence RICHARD DICKEN,   Ths. Slaughter
       JOHN LEWIS, BENJAMIN DICKEN
At a Court held for Culpeper County the 19th of Octr 1778 This Indenture ordered to be recorded.

pp.   THIS INDENTURE made the 15th of February in Reign of our Sovereign Lord
60-   George III 1776 Between ALEXANDER SPOTSWOOD Esquire of one part and PHILIP
63   DRAKE Witnesseth that said Alexander Spotswood for Rents and Covenants here-
           in after mentioned on part of said Philip Drake hath granted to farm let unto
Philip Drake Two hundred and sixty eight acres of land (except mines, minerals and quarries) being in the Parish of St. Marks in the County of Culpeper on the North side of the River Rappidanne being part of a Tract of Forty thousand acres left to said Alexander Spotswood by his Grandfather the bounds and limites of which Two hundred and sixty eight acres of land are described by a Plot & Survey thereof endorsed on the back of this Indenture To Hold the said Land to the said Philip Drake dureing the natural lifes of Philip Drake his Wife ANN DRAKE and PETER LERUE and longest liver of them paying yearly Eleven hundred pounds of Tobacco and Cask on the 25th of December and the said Philip Drake will within four years plant three hundred good Fruit trees one third at least to be good Apple trees and inclose the same within a good fence
Presence JOHN CRAIG,   Alexr. Spotswood
       JAMES LEWIS, BEN. BURBRIDGE,

WM. STROTHER, ALLEN WILEY, ROBT. DAWSON
At a Court held for Culpeper County the 15th of July 1776
This Indenture was partly proved by the Oaths of JAMES LEWIS and WILLIAM STROTHER
and ordered to be Certified. And at a Court held for the said County the 19th of October
1778 was fully proved by the Oath of Allen Wiley another Witness and ordered to be
recorded.

pp.   THIS INDENTURE made the 11th of March 1778 Between JOHN BROILE and
64-   MARGARET his Wife and ZACKARIAS BROILE and DELILAH his Wife of the Parish
66   of Bromfield County of Culpeper of one part and ANTHONY BERRY of Parish and
         County aforesaid Witnesseth that said John Broile and Margaret his Wife and
Zacharias Broile and Delilah his Wife for sum of Fifty five pounds current money hath
granted to said Anthony Berry his heirs forever Two hundred acres of land being part
of a Pattent granted to JACOB BROILE for Four hundred acres 28th September 1728 and
bounded Begining at two water oaks standing in a branch Corner to PETER BROILE
thence with his line to two white oaks on the side of a mountain & thence South to a
large white oak by a branch in NICHOLAS CRIGLERs line thence with his line South to a
Dead pine Corner to BURDINE thence North to the begining . . . .
Presence AM. BOHANNON,   John I B Broile
         ACREY BERRY, ADAM CLORE   Margaret W Broile
         CONRITE WILHOIT   Zacharias Z B Broile
                                                              Delilah D B Broile
   At a Court held for Culpeper County the 19th of Oct 1778
This Indenture was proved by the Oaths of Am. Bohannon, Acrey Berry and Adam Clow
and ordered to be recorded.

pp.   On margin: D. D. to Self
66-   THIS INDENTURE made the 19th day October 1777 Between JONAS MANIFEE and
69   ELISABETH his Wife of County of Culpeper of one part and JNO. FRANCIS LUCUS
         JACOBY of said County Witnesseth that Jonas Manifee and Elisabeth his Wife for
the sum Forty five pound Virginia Money hath granted unto said Jno. Francis Lucus
Jacoby and his heirs forever land in County of Culpeper and bounded Begining at a
Chesnut and white oak at a Corner of WILLIAM MANIFEEs thence North to two Chesnut
oaks to make a Dividing line betwixt GARRIOT and JONES thence said line continued
North still continued South to a white oak in NICHOLAS BATTAILs line thence with said
line South East still continued along said line South East to a white oak still with said
Battails line South to a Poplar and Dogwood Corner of Battails and William Manifees
thence along Manifee.s line N. to the beginning containing two hundred and ten acres . .
                                                              Jonas Manifield
   At a Court held for Culpeper County the 19th October 1778   Elizabeth Manifield
This Indenture from Jonas Manifee and Elisabeth his Wife ordered
to be recorded Previous to which the ssid Elizabeth was first privily examined
according to Law.

pp.   THIS INDENTURE made the 19th of October 1778 Between RICHARD NALLE and
69-   JUDITH his Wife of County of Culpeper & Parish of Bromfield of one part and
72   JOHN KENDALL of said County Witnesseth that said Richard Nalle and Judith his
         Wife for sum of Fifty pounds current money of Virginia have granted unto John
Kendall his heirs Four hundred acres of land in Culpeper County and Bromfield Parish
in the Goardvine Fork of Rappahannock River joining on the lower side GIANTS CASTLE
MOUNTAIN the same being a tract granted to said Richard Nalle by Deed from the Pro-

prietors Office dated the fourth day of September 1758 and said land is bounded
Begining at two pines on a hill side standing on the line of a Pattent granted to COLO.
HENRY WILLIS deceased now RICHARD THOMAS's and runing then North to a hikory
saplin on the side of the North end of GIANTS CASTLE MOUNTAIN thence North East to
three pines standing in or near said Richard Thomas's line thence with his line West to
the begining . . . .

                   Richd. Nalle
 At a Court held for Culpeper County the 19th October 1778   Judy Nalle
This Indenture ordered to be recorded Previous to which the
said Judy was first privily examined according to Law.

pp. THIS INDENTURE made the 20th of August 1773 Between JOHN McCARTY of County
72- of Culpeper of one part and JOHN LAWLOR of same County Witnesseth that said
75   John McCarty for sum Sixty five pounds Current money of Virginia hath sold
    unto said John Lawlor his heirs Two hundred and forty acres of land in Culpeper
County and Bromfield Parish on the branches of Cannons River in the Little Fork of
Rappahannock River the same being Two hundred acres of land purchased by said
John McCarty of JAMES COMPTON Esqr. and being part of Ten thousand acres granted to
said Compton by the right Honourable THOMAS LORD FAIRFAX Proprietor of the Nor-
thern Neck in Virginia and said Two hundred acres is bounded Begining at two Poplars
Corner to THOMAS PEYTON and runs thence South to a hikory on AARONS MOUNTAIN
thence South to a Hikory in a bottom thence North to three red oaks in Peytons line
thence with his line to the begining place To hold the said Two hundred and forty
acres . . . .
Presence CHARLES MOZINGO,   John McCarty
   WM. DUNCAN JR., WILLIAM DUNCAN, Younger
 At a Court held for Culpeper County the 15th of August 1774
This Indenture was partly proved by the Oath of Charles Mozingo one of the Witnesses
thereto & ordered to be Certified, And at a Court held for the said County the 19th day of
October 1778 was fully proved by the Oaths of William Duncan jr., and William Duncan
Yr. the other witnesses and ordered to be recorded.

pp. On margin: Delivd. to PIERCE 1796
75- THIS INDENTURE made the 19th of October 1778 Between JOHN KENDALL and
78   MARY his Wife of County of Culpeper and Parish of Bromfield of one part and
    JOHN PIERCE of County aforesd. Witnesseth that said John Kendall and Mary his
Wife for sum of Forty pounds current money of Virginia have granted unto John Pierce
one hundred and fifty acres of land in Culpeper County and Bromfield Parish in the
Gourdvine Fork of Rappahannock River joining on the lower side GIANTS CASTLE
MOUNTAIN the same being part of Four hundred acres of land granted to RICHARD
NALLE JUNR. by the right Honourable THOMAS LORD FAIRFAX Proprietor of the
Northern Neck in Virginia by Deed from the Proprietors Office dated the 4th day of
September 1750 and said land is bounded Begining at two pines Corner to RICHARD
THOMAS & ALEXANDER BURK on a spur of the South Giants Castle Mountain & running
thence with said Thomas's line East to three small oak saplings corner to JOSHUA
BROWNING thence with his line North to three red oaks in or near Thomas's line thence
North to a red oak in a line of Richard Nalles Deed thence with that line to the begining
. . . . .   John Kendall
 At a Court held for Culpeper County the 19th of October 1778 Molly Kendall
This Indenture ordered to be recorded Previous to which the
said Mary was first privily examined according to Law.

pp.   THIS INDENTURE made the 19th of October 1778 Between JOHN KENDALL and
78-   MOLLEY his Wife of the County of Culpeper and Parish of Bromfield of one part
81   and JOSHUA BROWNING of County aforesaid Witnesseth that said John Kindall
         and Molley his Wife for the sum Twenty seven pounds Ten shillings current
money of Virginia doth grant unto said Joshua Browning his heirs One hundred acres
of land in Culpeper County and Bromfield Parish in the Goardvine Fork of the Rappahannock River on the Lower side of GIANTS CASTLE MOUNTAIN the same being part of
Four hundred acres of land granted to RICHD. NALLE by the right Honourable THOMAS
LORD FAIRFAX Proprietor of the Northern Neck in Virginia by Deed from the Proprietors Office dated the fourth day of September 1750 as by said Deed will appear and said
One hundred acres is bounded Begining at three pines in a line of RICHARD THOMAS's
land and running with that line South to three red oaks in or near the said Thomas's
line thence with his line to the begining . . . .

John Kendall
Molly Kendall

   At a Court held for Culpeper County the 19th of October 1778
This Indenture ordered to be recorded Previous to which the
said Mary was first privily examined according to Law.

pp.   The Commonwealth of Virginia to THOMAS JOHNSTON, JOHN POINDEXTER and
81-   WADDY THOMPSON Gent. Whereas THOMAS JOHNSTON and ELISABETH his Wife of
82   the County of LOUISA by their Indenture of Bargain and Sale dated the 20th day
         of May 1776 have sold unto ADAM BANKS One thousand and seventy six acres of
land in Culpeper County and amongst the GREAT MOUNTAINS and Whereas the said
Elisabeth cannot conveniently travel to our County Court of Culpeper to make acknowledgement of the said conveyance we do command you that you go to the said Elisabeth
and examine her apart from her husband whether she be willing the same should be
recorded in our County Court and that she acknowledges the same without his threats
and when you have examined her that you Certifie us in our Court thereof. Witness
JOHN JAMESON Clerk this 8th day of Augt 1777
   Louisa Sct By virtue of this Writ we have examined Elisabeth privily and apart from
her husband who relinquished all her right of Dower to the land and declared she was
willing the same should be recorded in Court of Culpeper County and that she did it
freely without any force. Witness our hands this 12th day of May 1778.

THOMAS JOHNSTON   JN. POINDEXTER

   At a Court held for Culpeper County the 19th of October 1778
This Commission was retd. & ordered to be recorded.
See the Deed Recorded in Book H folio

pp.   On margin: D D 1791
83-   THIS INDENTURE made the 19th of October 1778 Between BENJA. SMITH of
85   County of Culpeper of one part and ADAM BANKS of aforesaid County Witnesseth
         that for sum Two hundred and fifty pounds current money of Virginia said
Benjamin Smith have sold unto said Adam Banks his heirs forever Two hundred and
sixty four acres of land lying on the Waters of the Rappidan River and bounded Begining at two red oaks in ISAAC SMITHs Plantation Corner to WILL STANTON thence
with said Stantons line South to a chesnut oak on the point of a Mountain thence East to
three Chesnutt oaks on the Top of the GERMAN RIDGE thence keeping the top and
running with an arm of the said Ridge East to the begining . . . .
Presence JNO. HUME,   Benja. ∫ Smith
   ISAAC SMITH, ISAAC Ɇ SMITH,
   DOWG. ⊥ SMITH

At a Court held for Culpeper County the 19th of October 1778
This Indenture ordered to be recorded.

pp.   THIS INDENTURE made this 20th day of July 1778 Between JAMES PENDLETON and
85-   CATHARINE his Wife of one part and JAMES ARNOLD of County of Culpeper Wit-
87   nesseth that said James Pendleton and Catharine his Wife for sum Twenty five
      pounds current money of Virginia have granted unto James Arnold his heirs a
parcel of land in the No. Little Fork of Rappahannock River and County aforesaid on
the Branches of Indian Run bounded Begining at a pine Corner of HANKINSON, READ
and WILLIS's old Survey running with Pendletons line South West to one white oak
saplin on the East side the RIDGE PATH thence running the several courses of the sd
Path South to two pines on the West side said Path in WILLIAM BOWMERs line thence
with his line North to three white oaks Corner of said Bowmer and Read thence with
Reads line North to the begining containing One hundred and fifty two acres . . . .

                                                          James Pendleton
At a Court held for Culpeper County the 19th of October 1778   Catharine Pendleton
This Indenture ordered to be recorded.

pp.   On margin: D D WM. SMITH 1792
87-   THIS INDENTURE made the 19th of October 1778 Between ISAAC SMITH of County
88   of Culpeper of one part and MALLINDER SMITH of County aforesaid of other part
      Witnesseth that said Isaac Smith for sum Five pounds have sold unto the said
Millander Smith her heirs land containing one hundred acres and bounded begining at
a Corner of WILLIAM RUCKERs on the ROAD that is a white oak thence to the head of a
branch to a Corner thence down the several courses to said Run to the river thence up
the severall courses of said River to a stony Clift and two pines from thence a straight
course to a pine on the aforementioned road thence several courses of ye said road to
the begining . . . .
                                                          Isaac Smith
At a Court held for Culpeper County the 19th of October 1778
This Indenture ordered to be recorded.

pp.   THIS INDENTURE made this 20th day of October 1778 Between BASSIL NOOE of
88-   County of Culpeper of one part and JOSHUA LINDSAY of County of Culpeper of
90   other part Witnesseth that said Basil Nooe for sum Two hundred pounds in hand
      paid do grant unto the said Joshua Lindsay his heirs One hundred and forty six
acres of land and bounded begining at a Double pine on the side of Beautiful Run the
West Fork of the above said Smiths Run near to the mouth of a small branch in a piece
of low ground and formerly a corner to two small tracts of land called DOWNERs and
SHELTONs thence along the Divideing line between the said Downer & Shelton to a road
called CAVES OLD ROAD thence along the said Old Road towards WILLIAM PENDLETONs
land to a Spanish Oak Corner in a line run by CAPT. JAMES WALKER for SAMUEL
SCRATCHWELL thence along the said line to a small branch which runs thro the Plantation formerly called Downers and Emptys into Smiths Run where Isaac Smiths MILL
FRAME to lay thence down the said Run to the mouth of Smiths Run thence up the said
Run to the Fork thence up the West Fork called Beautiful Run to the begining the other
tract containing Fifty acres Begining at the mouth of a branch in VERNONS MILL DAM
thence up the said branch to WILLIAM PENDLETONs line with his line to another
branch which heads in Pendletons Plantation thence down the said branch to where it
empties into said MILL DAM thence down the West of said Mill Dam to the begining

which land was conveyed unto said DEERING by RICHARD VERNON . . . .

                                                                Basil Nooe

At a Court held for Culpeper County the 20th October 1778
This Indenture ordered to be recorded.

pp.   On margin: D D to DAVID JAMESON May 1784
90-   THIS INDENTURE made this 16th day of November 1778 Between THOMAS THREL-
92   KELD of County of Culpeper & NELLY his Wife of one part and MOSES THRELKELD
           of County aforesaid Witnesseth that said Thomas Threlkeld and Nelly his Wife for
sum Three hundred and fifty pounds current money of Virginia have granted unto the
said Moses Threlkeld his heirs land in Parish of St. Marks & County of Culpeper bounded
Begining at three pines corner to FAIRFAX and YANCEY thence along Mr. COLEMANs
line East to two white oak Saplins Corner to STEVENS, thence with his line South to two
hickories Corner to EDWARD MOORE thence with his line to the back line of REYNOLDS
to two red oaks with that line to the Begining being the ballance of land purchased by
Thomas Threlkeld of JOHN REYNOLDS containing Eighty eight acres of land . . . .

                                                                Thomas Threlkeld
At a Court held for Culpeper County the 16th day of Novr. 1778   Nelly Threlkeld
This Indenture ordered to be recorded, Previous to which the
said Nelly was first privily examined according to Law.

pp.   On margin: D D to MR. FITZPATRICK Augt 20th 1780
92-   THIS INDENTURE Witnesseth that JOSEPH WOOD and ELISABETH his Wife of Cul-
93   peper County for divers good causes and Paternal Affection they do bear to
           MARY WOOD Relict of their Son JOHN SCOTT WOOD late of said County deceased and
their three children ELIABETH WOOD, JUDITH WOOD & JAMES WOOD hath given the use
of one parcel of land in the County of Culpeper and being the land whereon the said
Mary Wood now Dwelleth and bounded Begining at a red oak and two white oaks Corner
to BARBOUR SCOTT and JOSEPH WOOD runing thence with said Woods line North East to
three pines and two red oaks on a RIDGE PATH thence South to Deep Branch thence
down the said Branch binding on the same to the mouth at two poplars on the South side
of Beaverdam Run thence South to a pine on the MILL PATH thence South to SCOTTs line
thence with said line to the begining the said land containing One hundred and
seventy seven acres . . . In Witness we have set our hands this 16 November 1778.

                                                                Joseph Wood
At a Court held for Culpeper County the 16th November 1778   Elisa. Wood
This Indenture ordered to be recorded, Previous to which the sd
Elisa. was first privily exd. according to Law.

pp.   THIS INDENTURE made this 16th November 1778 Between SAMUEL CLAYTON JUNR
94-   Surviving Executor of AMBROSE CAMP Deceased of one part and ROBERT LATHAM
95   Infant and heir at Law of JOSEPH LATHAM Decd of other part. Whereas said Am-
           brose Camp by his Last Will and Testament recorded in County Court of Culpeper
did desire his Executors to sell Two hundred acres of land which he purchased of Mr.
GEORGE WETHERALL and the money arising to be applyed towards discharging his just
debts in Pursuance of said Will the Executor did sell the said land to Joseph Latham who
soon after departed this Life (before any acknowledgment could be made) haveing no
issue of his Body and this said Robert Latham Son of JOHN LATHAM deceased the Elder
Brother of said Joseph now becomes Heir at Law NOW THIS INDENTURE WITNESSETH that
for the sum Fifty pounds Current money to them paid he the said Samuel Clayton Junr.
Surviving Executor of the said Ambrose Camp Deceased by these presents do grant unto

the said Robert Latham his heirs Two hundred acres of land in County aforesaid and bounded Begining at three white oaks Corner to ROWE thence South to two red oak Saplins on a branch thence South to two white oak Saplins in the Fork of Priors Branch from thence to the begining . . . .

Presence JOHN WAUGH,   Sam Clayton jr.
          PHILIP PENDLETON, MASON COLVIN
   At a Court held for Culpeper County the 16th of November 1778
This Indenture ordered to be recorded.

pp.   On margin: D. D. DANL. PALMER 1797
96-   THIS INDENTURE made this 15th day of November 1778 Between OBADIAH
97   WRIGHT and HANNAH WRIGHT Wife of the said Obadiah of Culpeper County of
         one part and JOSEPH PARMER of STAFFORD COUNTY Witnesseth Know ye that we
the said Obadiah Wright and wife hath this day sold to said Joseph Parmer Two hundred acres of land in Culpeper County ye little fork of Rappahannock River Bounded Begining on the North River at the Mouth of a small branch between JAMES GRIMSLEY and said land at a white oak East to three white oaks one of which is marked thus on ye point of a ridge thence West in one other of ye said Grimsleys lines thence South to one pine Corner to JONATHAN FREEMAN thence South to one pine on the side of JOBERS MOUNTAIN thence East to red oaks Corner to said Freeman thence South to three pines Corner to Green thence a straight course to ye Beging. line dividing Between said land of HARMON VISCARVERs thence with said Viscarvers line to a small branch where JNO. HOPPERS FORD crosses ye North River thence up said river to ye Begining to ye only proper use of ye said Joseph Parmer his heirs forever free from the hindrance of us our heirs for ye consideration of one hundred pounds current money of Virginia . . .
                                                                    Obadiah Wright
   At a Court held for Culpeper County the 16th of   Hannah Wright
November 1778 This Indenture ordered to be recorded Previous
to which the said Hannah was first privily examined according to Law.

pp.   On margin: D Nov 20th 1780
97-   THIS INDENTURE made the 8th day October 1778 Between LEAH MITCHELL Relict
100   of JACOB MITCHELL late deceased and JAMES THOMAS & THOMAS ALLEN Executors
         of the Last Will and Testament of said Jacob Mitchell Deceased and residents of
County of Culpeper of one part and AMBROSE GREENHILL of ESSEX COUNTY of other part Witnesseth that said Leah Mitchell, James Thomas and Thomas Allen for sum One hundred and thirty pounds current money do sell unto said Ambrose Greenhill and his heirs land in Culpeper County on the North side of the Cabin Branch according to a survey thereof is as followeth Begining at a white and red oak Corner to other lands of said Leah Mitchell and also Corner to ROBERTSONs Lott whence with said Lott South to two box oaks near Cabin Branch thence down the branch the several courses to two Willow oaks Corner to other lands of said Ambrose Greenhill thence with his line North to two Spanish Oak saplins and one pine Corner to said Leah Mitchell thence with her line to the begining containing forty six acres . . . .

                                                                    Leah + Mitchell
   At a Court held for Culpeper County the 16th of November   James Thomas
1788 This Indenture ordered to be recorded.   Thomas Allen

pp.   THIS INDENTURE made the 16th of November 1778 Between BENJAMIN PETTY and
100-   MARTHA PETTY his Mother of the County of Culpeper of one part and WILLIAM
102   ROBERTS of County aforesaid Witnesseth that said Benjamin Petty and Martha

Petty for sum of One hundred pounds current money of Virginia hath granted unto the said William Roberts his heirs forever One hundred and fifty eight acres of land in the County aforesaid in the Fork of the Rappidan and Robertson Rivers and is bounded Begining at two pines near the Three Prong Branch and in a line of FLINTs and Corner to BENJAMIN HAINES and runing with his line South to the Three Prong Branch thence up the several courses of said Branch to a white oak Corner to Flint thence North to a Scrubby white oak Corner to Flint in a line of AMBROSE POWELLS thence East to HAYNES Corner in a line of Ambrose Powells thence with his line to the begining containing One hundred and fifty eight acres of land . . . .

                                                      Benjamin Petty
    At a Court held for Culpeper County the 16th day of   Martha Petty
November 1778 This Indenture ordered to be recorded
Previous to which the said Martha was first privily examined according to Law.

pp.   On margin: D. D. to Self 86
102-   THIS INDENTURE made the 16th day of November 1778 Between JAMES McDANIEL
105   of County of Culpeper Painter and MARY his Wife of one part and WILLIAM
        CRISEL of said County Planter of other part Witnesseth that said James McDanl.
and Mary his Wife for the sum Thirty pounds current money to them paid hath granted unto the said William Crisel his heirs forever a supposed Quantity of Thirty acres of land which was conveyed to the said McDaniel by TIMOTHY HOLDWAY Begining at Holdways third Pattent line at a pine and Chesnut a South Southeast Course up the Mountain to a Chesnut oak on the top of the Mountain thence Northeast to the begining . . . .
Presence TIMY. HOLDWAY,   James McDaniel
    ELIJAH SIMMS   Mary ⅄ McDaniel
    At a Court held for Culpeper County the 16th of November 1778
This Indenture ordered to be recorded Previous to which the said Mary was first privily examined according to Law.

pp.   On margin: D. D. GEORGE CHRISTLER 1785
105-   THIS INDENTURE made the Sixteenth day of November 1778 Between HENRY
106   CHRISTLER and ELISABETH his Wife of County of Culpeper of one part and
        SAMUEL ROUSE of aforesaid County Witnesseth that for sum Seventy pounds
current money of Virginia the said Henry Christler have sold unto the said Samuel Rouse his heirs forever One hundred acres of land in County of Culpeper Begining at three pines Corner in a line of GEO. BUMGARDNERs Decd and runing thence South to a Scrubby Oak in PETER WEAVERs line thence with said Weavers line South East to three red oaks in WILLIAM JETTs line thence with said Jetts line to the Begining . . . .
                                                      Henry Christler
    At a Court held for Culpeper County the 16th of November   Elisa. Christler
1778 This Indenture ordered to be recorded, Previous to
which the said Elisa. was first privily examined according to Law.

pp.   THIS INDENTURE made the 27th of October 1778 Between JAMES HENSON & CATT his
107-   Wife of County of Culpeper and Parish of Bromfield of one part and ROBERT
108   McALLESTER of the same County and Parish Witnesseth that the aforesaid James
        Henson and Catt his Wife for the sum Forty five pounds current money have sold
unto him the said Robert McAllester his heirs all that land whereon James Henson now lives being in the aforesaid County and Parish and on the Waters of Pophams Run and is bounded Begining on the North side of Pophams Run near the WIDOW McALLESTERs and joining SAMPSONs line thence with his line so far as FINLA McALLESTERs line the

said Sampsons to the North of said Run thence up said Finlaes line to the land said Finla
gave the said James Henson and Catt his Wife thence with theirs & CHARLES HENSONs
line to said Pophams Run thence down the said Run to the begining containing seventy
acres of land and includes the land the said James Henson and Catt his Wife by the said
Finla McAllester above mentd. and the land bought by said James Henson of WILLIAM
McALLESTER the bounds of record in the County Court of Culpeper . . . .
Presence BENJAMIN LILLARD,   James ⫱ Henson
      GEO. WITHERALL, RIGINAL BURDINE   Catt ◯ Henson
      WILLIAM HENSON
  At a Court held for Culpeper County the 16th of Novr. 1778
This Indenture ordered to be recorded.

pp.   THIS INDENTURE made the 17th day of August 1778 Between JOHN BARNHISLE
109-   and FRANCES his Wife of County of Culpeper of one part and BENJAMIN STINNETT
111   of County aforesaid Witnesseth that for sum of Eighty five pounds current
       money of Virginia they have granted unto the said Benjamin Stinnett One hun-
dred and sixty five acres of land in Culpeper County on the branches of Blackwater Run
and is bounded Begining at two white oaks in COLEMANs old line and runs thence South
to three small Maples on the bank of North Fork of the aforesaid Blackwater Run near
the ROAD thence South to three black oaks on a ridge in Colemans line thence with the
line South to three small Chesnut oaks on the West side of the RED OAK MOUNTAIN
thence to the begining . . . .
Presence BEN PULLIAM,   John Barn ⊗ hisle
      WILLIAM ALLAN, WILLIAM JONES   Frances 𝒻 Hisle
  At a Court held for Culpeper County the 16th of November 1778
This Indenture ordered to be recorded, Previous to which the said Frances was first
privily examined according to Law.

pp.   On margin: D. D. to JAS. LILLARD 22d Apl. 1780
111-   THIS INDENTURE made this 30th day of October 1778 Between ADAM GAAR of the
113   County of Culpeper of one part and JAMES LILLARD of the County aforesaid Wit-
       nesseth that said Adam Gaar for the sum Three hundred pounds current money
of Virginia have sold unto said James Lillard his heirs the fee simple Estate of Two hundred acres of land in the County aforesaid bounded Begining at one red oak on the
South side of Hughes River and runs thence South to two Chesnuts on the side of the
RAGED MOUNTAIN thence South to one Chesnut Corner to JOHN GAAR near to THOMAS
JINKINS Dwelling house thence with said Gaars line to a poplar on the bank of the
aforesaid river thence up the several courses of said river to the begining . . . .
Presence of BENJAMIN LILLARD,
      ROBT. SHOTWELL, SAMUEL LEATHER,   Adam Gaar
      GEO. WITHERALL
  At a Court held for Culpeper County the 16th of November 1778
This Indenture with a Memorandum and Receipt Endorsed ordered to be recorded.

pp.   THIS INDENTURE made the 17th day of April 1778 Between SAMUEL LEATHERER
113-   and MARY his Wife of the County of Culpeper of one part and BENJAMIN LIL-
115   LARD of the County aforesaid Witnesseth that the said Samuel Leatherer and
       Mary his Wife for the sum Fifteen pounds current money of Virginia have
granted unto the said Benjamin Lillard his heirs a parcel of land containing three
acres and three quarters in the County aforesaid and bounded Begining at a chesnut
Corner to JAMES GARRIOTT and runeth thence North to a Dogwood by a ROAD thence

South to a white oak on the said Road thence to the begining . . . .
Presence of JAMES GARRIOTT,   Samuel Leatherer
    JOHN BRADLEY, JAMES YOWELL,   Mary Leatherer
    JOHN CROW
  At a Court held for Culpeper County the 16th day of November 1778
This Indenture with a Memorandum and Receipt Endorsed ordered to be recorded.

pp.   THIS INDENTURE made the Sixteenth day of Novr. 1778 Between BRYANT
115-   McGRATH and MARY his Wife of the County of Culpeper of one part and JOHN
118   PRIEST of the County aforesaid Witnesseth that said Bryant McGrath and Mary
     his Wife for sum of Thirty five pounds Current money of Virginia have granted
unto the said John Priest his heirs One hundred and ten acres of land in Culpeper
County and Bromfield Parish in the Great Fork of the Rappahannock River joining on
the Northeast side the MAIN RED OAK MOUNTAIN & bounded Begining at three red oaks
Corner to JAMES WILLIAMS and runs thence North to a white oak in JOHN BARRCILES
line thence with his line South to three red oaks Corner to Barrcile and BIRKETT
DAVENPORT thence with Davenports line South to a Locust Corner to Davenport in a
hallow of the Red Oak Mountain near a large Rock thence with another of Davenports
lines South West to a hikory on a Ridge of the said Mountain East to two Spanish Oaks in
or near a line of James Williams thence with Williams line to the begining . . . .
                                            Bryant Magrath
At a Court held for Culpeper County the 16th of November 1778   Mary Magrath
This Indenture ordered to be recorded Previous to which the
said Mary was first privily examined according to Law.

pp.   THIS INDENTURE made the 15th day November 1778 Between JAMES BALLENGER
118-   and DARCUS his Wife of the County of Culpeper of one part and BENJAMIN
121   THRELKELD of the County of FAUQUIER of other part Witnesseth that said James
     Ballenger and Darcus his Wife for sum One hundred and fifty pounds current
money of Virginia have granted unto the said Benjamin Threlkeld his heirs forever a
parcel of land in the said County of Culpeper and being a parcel of land which the said
James Ballenger had of JOHN THRELKELD Begining at a forked Chesnut and chesnut oak
on the top of the BLUE RIDGE Corner to land of DADE and runing thence leaving his line
No. to a white oak on the North side of the said Ridge opposite to DICKEYS HILL thence
South to three hikories on the South side of the Blue Ridge thence South to three chesnuts in a great Bottom called SASSAFRAS THICKETT thence North West to Dades Corner
the same courses continued to the begining containing Four hundred and five acres of
land . . . .
                                       James Ballenger
  At a Court held for Culpeper County the 16th of November 1778
This Indenture Ordered to be recorded Previous to which the said Darcus was first
privily examined according to Law.

p.   I Hereby impower MR. THOMAS JORDAN to Collect the Rents due from the Cul-
122   peper Estate in the same manner as he has heretofore been entitled to do. In
    Witness I have hereunto set my hand & Seal
Teste JOHN STROTHER,   Peter Presly Thornton
    JN. CATESBY COCKE
  At a Court held for Culpeper County the 16th of November 1778
This Power of Attorney was proved by the Oath of John Catesby Cocke & ordered to be
recorded.

pp. On margin: D D to DAY 18 Mar 83
122- THIS INDENTURE made this Seventh day of November 1778 Between THOMAS
124 SCOTT of CAROLINE COUNTY of one part and AMBREE DAY of Culpeper County of
the other part Witnesseth that the said Thomas Scott for the sum Fifty pounds
current money of Virginia doth release the said Ambree Day his heirs He the said Thomas Scott have granted unto the said Ambree Day his heirs a track or parcell of land in Culpeper County containing six hundred and ninety four acres and is bounded by the lines of EDWIN HICKNAN, PRESLEY THORNTON and FRANCIS BROWNING it being a parcel of land the said Thomas Scott and GEORGE WILEY purchased in partnership and said Wiley by these presents freely consents to the Sail hereof to hold the said six hundred and ninety four acres of land and Lastly the said Thomas Scott and MARTHA his Wife there heirs hereby granted unto said Ambree Day his heirs for ever against them the said Thomas Scott and Martha his Wife . . . .

Presents JOHN WILEY,   Thomas Scott
    PHILIP JOHNSON, NICHOLAS JOHNSON   George Wiley

  At a Court held for Culpeper County the 16th of November 1778
This Indenture was proved as to Thomas Scott by the Witnesses thereto and was acknowledged by the said GEORGE WILEY and ordered to be recorded.

pp. On margin: D. D. 1793
125- KNOW ALL MEN by these presents that I JAMES YAWELL Son of DAVID YAWELL
126 of Culpeper County for Covenants and Reserves hereinafter mentioned have
consented that as my Father David Yawell did sometime pass (by Deed of Gift which recourse being had to the records of the County Court of Culpeper will more fully appear) do Bargain Sell and deliver all my right to my Brother DAVID YAWELL in one Negroe wench named Bett one of the Negroes in the Deed of Gift above mentioned and one equal share of all other things in the Deed of Gift mentioned be the said David Yawell in every respect being oblig'd to perform the one half of all that I by the said Deed am compelled to, and shall in every respect do his full and equal share of the parts whereon I am by the said Deed compelled to do, Provided never the less, if said David will on only two days notice pay to him the same James Yawell the sum of Three hundred pounds or from time to time as said James shall suffer with all cost and damages that said James shall suffer that then he the said David to be and have full Right to the Negroe and Things above as I have, but if he the said David should fail to do and perform the things above then this to be void or else in full force and Virtue the 17th day of Sept 1778.

                        James Yawell
by consent of the above parties 'tis hereafter to be Call'd   David X Yawell
mutual in the parties to these presents to have fixed their hands and
seals the day and date consequence whereof mutually above mentioned
    ROBT. SHOTWELL, GEORGE WETHERALL,
    JAMES X YAWELL, SAMUEL LEATHER
  At a Court held for Culpeper County the 16th of November 1778
This Deed was proved and Ordered to be recorded.

pp. On margin: D. D. 1790
126- KNOW ALL MEN by these presents that we DAVID YAWELL and JAMES YAWELL
128 Son of the said David have mutually agreed with each other for and in behalf of
him the said David Intermarrying with MARTHA TOMBLINS by and with the consent of his said son James and that the same more fully appear aforesaid David gave up his whle Estate to the said James with this Proviso that he would suport and maintain

him in a resonble manner during his natual life and the same is of record in County
Court of Culpeper bearing date the - d - 1776 and now since the said Intermarriage he
the said James has given up several articles which is in the actual possession of him the
said David which he and his Wife Martha is to have and enjoy during their natural lives
provided said Martha should not Intermarry with some person beside the said David
Yawell her present husband but in case she should intermary at the demise of the said
David that then she have one equal share of all said David shall possess at his demise
and to enjoy same dureing her natural life and at her demise dispose of the same as she
may see cause amongst the children of her Son in Law James and her Son in Law David
and in the meantime the said James does promise with said David and Martha that he
will during their natual lives support them in their distress as was formely agreed on
by said James and said David during his Life in Witness the parties have set their hands
& seals the 17th day of Sept 1778.
Presents of ROBT. SHOTWELL,   David X Yawell
    SAMUEL LEATHER, JAMES X YAWELL,   James Yawell
    GEO. WETHERALL
  At a Court held for Culpeper County the 16th of Novr. 1778
This Deed ordered to be record'd.

pp.   On margin: D. D. to PHIL. CLAYTON 15th Sept 84
128- THIS INDENTURE made this 25th day of April 1777 Between JOHN WILLIS and
132- SARAH his Wife of the Parish of St. Thomas and County of ORANGE of one part
    and JOHN ROGERS of St. Marks Parish and County of Culpeper of other part Wit-
nesseth that John Willis and Sarah his Wife for the sum Two hundred and fifty pounds
current money to them paid do grant unto the said John Rogers his heirs all that Track
of land in the Parish of St. Mark and County of Culpeper being a track of land wiled to
the said John Willis by his Father JOHN WILLIS reference to sd Will recorded in Orange
Court and the several Deeds of conveyances to wit from SPOTSWOOD to WAUGH. and from
WAUGH to Willis Spotswood to Willis recorded in the County Court of Culpeper will make
the title more fully appear and it is bounded Begining at two white oaks Corner to
JAMES WILLIS in SAMUEL REEDs line thence with his line South to a pine in a line of
DANIEL WHITEs thence with his line thence North to a white oak in the Low grounds of
Ceadar Run thence down the run to a Walnut Tree in the South side thereof Corner to
James Willis thence leaving the said Run South to the begining containing two
hundred and eighty five acres of land . . . .
Presence JAMES PENDLETON,   John Willis
    JOHN WAUGH, JOHN WILLIAMS JUR.   Sarah Willis
  The Commonwealth of Virginia to NATHANIEL PENDLETON, JAMES PENDLETON and JOHN
WAUGH Gentlemen Whereas John Willis and Sarah his Wife have sold unto John Rogers
land on the South side of Ceder Run in the County of Culpeper and Whereas the said
Sarah cannot conveniently travil to our said County Court to make acknowledgement of
the said conveyances we give you power to go to the said Sarah and examine her purely
and apart from her husband and when you have receiv'd her acknowledgement that
you Certifie us thereof in our said Court. Witness JOHN JAMESON Clerk at the house of
the County the 25th day of April 1777
  Pursuant to the within Commission to us directed we did go to the said Sarah and examine her touching the acknowledgment of the within conveyance apart from her
husband and she declar'd she was willing said conveyance should be recorded. Witness
this 25th day of April 1777.
        JAMES PENDLETON   JOHN WAUGH

At a Court held for Culpeper County the 18th of August 1777
This Indenture was partly proved by the Oaths of James Pendleton and John Waugh
Witnesses theirto And at a Court held for the said County the 16th of Novr. 1778 was
fully proved by the Oaths of JOHN WILLIAMS JUNR. another Witness with a memorandum and reciept and Commission thereto annexed is ordered to be recorded.

pp.   THIS INDENTURE made the Sixteenth day of Novemr. 1778 Between ALEXANDER
132-   McDANALD of County of Culpeper of one part and JAMES WILLIS of the said
134   County Witnesseth that said Alexander McDANIEL for the sum Eight Hundred
     Poun have granted unto said James Willis his heirs for ever land in the County
of Culpeper containing Two hundred and fourteen acres it being purchased by the said
Alexander McDonal from RICHARD REYNOLDS & JOHN SPOTSWOOD Esqr. and is bounded
Begining at a Corner to FRANCIS LOWENS in an old field thence with his line South to a
white oak on Cedar Run Corner to said Lowens thence up the said Run the several
courses thereof to three white oaks Corner to Willis thence North to the begining . . . .
                                 Alexander McDonald

At a Court held for Culpeper County the 16th Novr. 1778
This Indenter ordered to be recorded.

pp.   THIS INDENTURE made the Sixth day of November 1778 Between JAMES WILLIS
134-   of the County of Culpeper and ANN his Wife of one part and ALEXANDER
137   McDONALD of said County Witnesseth that James Willis and Ann his Wife for the
     sum Four hundred pounds do hereby grant unto the said Alexander McDonald
his heirs for ever land in the County of Culpeper containing one hundred and forty
acres it being purchased by James Willis of JOHN WILLIS and is bounded Begining at
two white oaks on the South side of Cedar Run Corner to JOHN ROGERS thence down the
run North to an Elm standing on the South side of Cedar Run Corner to ANN WHITE
thence with her line South to four white oaks Corner to SAMUEL READs thence with his
line North to a chesnut tree on the South side of the run Corner to John Rogers thence
with his line down the run to the begining . . . .
                                 James Willis
At a Court held for Culpeper County the 16th Novr. 1778   Ann Willis
This Indenture ordered to be recorded, Previous to which the
said Ann was first privily Examined according to Law.

pp.   THIS INDENTURE made the Sixteenth day of November 1778 Between ADAM
137-   WILHOIT and BATEY his Wife of the County of Culpeper of one part and BRYANT
140   McGRATH of the County aforesaid Witnesseth that the said Adam Wilhoit and
     PATEY his Wife for the sum Sixty pounds current money of Virginia have sold
Fifty acres of land in Culpeper County and Bromfield Parish in the Great Fork of the
Rappahannock River and bounded Begining at two Chesnuts on a Mountain West to a
hickory on the top of the ridge of the said Mountain thence South to a red oak in the
West side of Deep Run thence West to two red oaks on a hill side Corner to land formaly
belonging to JOHN TOWLES thence North to the Begining place . . . .
                                 Adam Wilhoit
At a Court held for Culpeper County the 16th of Novr. 1778
This Indenture ordered to be recorded.

pp.   On margin: D. D. R. FLYNT 1786
140-   THIS INDENTURE made the Sixteenth day of Novr. 1778 Between JACOB NICELY
142   and MARGRET his Wife of the County of Culpeper of one part and SAMUEL KER-

SEY of the said County Witnesseth that said Jacob Nicely and Margret his Wife for the
sum Eighty pounds current money of Virginia have granted unto said Samuel Kersey
his heirs forever land in the County of Culpeper which was formerly sold by ROBERT
LEAVELL and SARAH his Wife to CHRISTIAN READMAN and since sold to the above sd
Jacob Nicely party to these presents and containing one hundred acres bounded
Begining at two pine on a hillside in AMBROSE POWELLs line runing thence South to
two white oaks near a branch in WILLIAM CROSWAITs line thence with his line North
crossing a Mountain to two white oaks on the West side thereof East to one red oak
saplin in a Valley near said Powels line thence East to the begining . . . .
Presence of JOSEPH WOOD   Jacob ✕ Nicely
         THOMAS SCOTT, PHILLIP WATERFIELD   Margret ✕ Nicely
   At a Court held for Culpeper County the 16th of Novr. 1778
This Indenture ordered to be recorded, Previous to which the said Margret was first
examined according to Law.

pp.   THIS INDENTURE made the tenth day of Novr 1778 Betwen EDMOND BROWNING
142-   and MARY his Wife of the County of Culpeper of one part and WILLIAM ROBERTS
144   of the same County Witnesseth that said Edmond Browning and Mary his Wife
         they do grant unto the said William Roberts his heirs a track of land containing
One hundred and seventy acres being part of the land purchased by ROGER DIXON of
WILLIAM RUSSELL and sold to sd Edmon Browning and bounded begining at a gum on
the South side of the Hedgman River at the Mouth of a little Branch thence to the sd
River to a hickory saplin on the river just about the cleared ground where JOHN NOR-
MAND liv'd thence South to a hickory in the said Dixons back line thence with that line
to the begining . . . .
Presence SAMUEL   Edmond Browning
       JAMES PENDLETON, BIRKETT DAVENPORT,   Mary Browning
       ROBERT SEALE
   At a Court held for Culpeper County the 16th day of Novr.1778
This Indenture was prove by the Oaths of SAMUEL FARGESON, PHILIP PENDLETON &
BIRKETT DAVENPORT Witnesses thereto and ordered to be recorded.

pp.   TO ALL TO WHOM these presents shall come Know Ye that DARBY CONNER and
144-   MARY CONNER of the County of ORANGE and State of NORTH CAROLINA for the
145   natural love which we bear unto our Mother ANN NASH of County of Culpeper
         and State of Virginia and for the sum Thirty pounds current money of Virginia
we have granted all our title to a negroe boy named Cyrus to be devided betwen Brother
BENJAMINE and ourselves and now in the possession of the said Ann Nash which said
right we do give to said Ann Nash this first day of December 1778.
Presence THOMAS BUTLER,   Darby Conner
       WILLIAM BUTLER   Mary Conner
   At a Court held for Culpeper County the 21st of December 1778
This Indenture Deed of Gift ordered to be recorded.

pp.   On margin; D. D. his Son WM. CAMPBELL 1805
145-   THIS INDENTURE made this 21st day of December 1778 Between JACOB WHEET-
147   MORE and ANN his wife of County of Culpeper of one part and OWEN CAMPBELL
         of County aforesaid Witnesseth that said Jacob Wheetmore and Ann his Wife for
sum of Six hundred and Sixty four pounds Eleven Shillings current money of Virginia
do sell unto the said Owen Campbell land in the County aforesaid containing two hundred and forty nine acres bounded Begining at two white oaks thence North to a red oak

near the Fork of the Road thence with CORNELIUS MITCHELL line South to a Gum in
OWEN MINORs line thence with his line South to a poplar Corner to PEARSON CHAPMAN
thence North to the Begining . . . . .
Presence of JOHN WIGGINTON

Jacob X Whitmore
Ann X Wheetmore

At a Court held for Culpeper County the 21st Decr. 1778
This Indenture ordered to be recorded Previous to which the said Anne was first privily
examined according to Law.

pp.   On margin: D. D. to WM. McQUEEN 3d June 1784
147-   TO ALL TO WHOM these presents shall come Know ye that I the sd ALEXANDER
148   McQUEEN of the County of Culpeper for the sum Five shillings Current money
        but more espicially for the natural love which I have for my son ALEXANDER
McQUEEN JUNER doth give unto my sd Son Alexander McQuinn junr and his heirs Four
hundred and ninety three acres of land being the track of land I now live being part of
an inclusive Deed granted to me from the LORD FAIRFAX bearing date the 28 June 1775
also Nine Negores (to wit) Simon, Phill, James, Mill, Luce, Rachel, George, Eve, Peter
with increase of said Mill Luce Rachel and Eve. I have set my hand and seal this 30 Day
of October 1778.
Presents PHILIP WATERFIELD,   Alexander McQueen
        JAMES WHITEHEAD, PHILEMAN YANCEY
At a Court held for Culpeper County the 21st day of December 1778
This Indented Deed of Gift ordered to be recorded.

pp.   On margin: D. D. to JNO. ROGERS 1787
148-   THIS INDENTURE made this third/fourth day of September 1778 Between
153   ALEXANDER DOYLE of the Town of DUMFRIES in the County of PRINCE WILLIAM
        and ELIZABETH DOYLE his Wife of one part and GEORGE WIRT of the County of
NEW CASTLE in the State of DELAWARE in the State of PENSYLVANIA of the other part
Witnesseth that for the sum of Two hundred pounds current money of Virginia paid to
the said Alexander Doyle and Elizabeth his Wife have sold unto the said George Wirt in
his actual possession by Virtue of the Statute for Transferring uses into possession all
that land containing Two hundred and fifty three acres in the County of Culpeper in
the Great Fork of Rappahannock River and is part of a track of land formerly granted
to a certain THOMAS STANTON Deceased and conveyed by GERRARD BANKS and ANN his
Wife to a certain JOHN BUTLER by Deeds of Lease and Release the 15th and 16th day of
November 1769 and by the said John Butler and Wife conveyed to the said Alexander
Doyle by Deeds of lease and release the 26 and 27 days of February 1776 and which
several Deeds are recorded among the records of the County Court of Culpeper . . . .
Presence of CHARLES ADAMS,   Alexander Doyle
        JOHN LANGFIT, EVAN WILLIAMS
At a Court held for Culpeper County the 15th of February 1779
This Indenture of Lease and Release together with the Commission thereto annexed is
ordered to be recorded.
The Commonwealth of Virginia to RICHARD GRAYHAM, REGINALD GRAHAM, WILLIAM
BRENT, JOHN MUERRY Gentl. Whereas Alexander Doyle and Elizabeth his Wife have sold
to George Wirt of State of Pensylvania land in the County of Culpeper and Whereas the
said Elizabeth cannot travel to our County Court to make acknowledgement of the said
conveyance we do give you power to go the said Elizabeth and examine her apart from
her husband whether she doth the same without his threats and when you have received her acknowledgement that you certify us thereof. Witness JOHN JAMESON Clerk

the Fourth day of September in the 3 year of the Commonweath 1778.

PRINCE WILLIAM Sct. In Obedience to the within Writ we the Subscribers two of the Justices of the peace for the County aforesaid have caused Elizabeth Doyle to come before us and have examined her privily who acknowledged that she executed the Deed of her own free will and is willing the same should be recorded in the Court of Culpeper. Witness this 21st day of Octr. 1778.

WILLIAM BRENT   JOHN MURRAY

pp. On margin: D D DANL. JAMES 1792. See Common recorded in P. 455
153- THIS INDENTURE made this Eight day of Feby 1779 Betwen WILLIAM SPARKS
155 ELIZABETH his Wife and RICHARD SEALES of the County of Culpeper of one part
and JOSEPH PORTER of the County aforesaid of the other part Witnesseth that for the sum Three hundred pounds current money of Virginia the sd William Sparks and Elizabeth his Wife and Richrd Seales have sold unto Joseph Porter his heirs for ever five acres of land in the County aforesaid and on the waters of the Robinson River and bounded Begining at a Cherry tree on Dark Run and on the South side of the said Run a little below an old MILL place thence up the several courses of the said run to the Begining . . . .

Presence of JOHN HUME,   William X Sparks
    JOSEPH HAYNS, ABSOLOM BOBO,   Elizabeth Sparks
    JAMES HAYNES, GEORGE SWINDLE,   Richard Seales
    JAMES SLAUGHTER, JOHN FITZPATRICK,
    SAMUEL HENING, JOHN WAUGH

At a Court held for Culpeper County the 15th day of Feby 1779 This Indenture with Memorandum and Receipt was ordered to be recorded & on the Motion of the said Porter a Commission is awarded for the private examination of the said Elizabeth which when the same was returned with a Certificate thereon is ordered to be recorded.

pp. On margin: D D CHS. BRUCE 1792
155- THIS INDENTURE made the 15th Feby 1779 Betwen EDWARD VAUS of County of
158 Culpeper and JEAN his Wife of one part and CHARLES BRUCE of County of
ORANGE of other part Witnesseth that said Edward Vaus and Jean his Wife for sum of Two hundred and sixty five pounds current money hath sold unto the said Charles Bruce his heirs for ever land in County of Culpeper containing one hundred and eighteen acres begining at an Elm on Potator Run thence South to no Corner mentioned thence North to a Box Oak Corner to BLOODWORTHs near ROGUES ROAD thence South to Corner mentioned at Rogues Road thence down the said Road to SPOTSWOODs line thence East to a spanish oak stump on Potator Run thence up the said run to the begining . . . .

Edward Vass

The Commonwealth of Virginia Whereas Edward Vass and JANE his Wife have sold unto Charles Bruce of County of Orange land in County of Culpeper and whereas the said Jane cannot travel to our County Court to make acknowledgement of the said conveyance we give unto you power to receive the acknowledgement which the said Jane shall be willing to make and when you have recorded her acknowledgement that you Certify us thereof in our said Court. Witness JOHN JAMESON Clerk this 19th day of January 1779 and the Fourth year of our Commonwealth.

At a Court held for Culpeper County the 15th of Feby 1779 This Indenture ordered to be recorded.

pp.   On margin: D. D. 20th Nov 1780
158-   THIS INDENTURE made this 14th day of February 1779 Betwen JOHN BUTTON and
159   SUSANNAH his Wife of County of Culpeper of one part and WILLIAM BUTTON of
        aforesaid County Witnesseth that said John Button and Susannah his Wife for
the sum of Five shillings Current money of Virginia sell unto said William Button One
hundred acres which said tract of land was granted to John Button Senor decd for one
hundred acres as by the Patent from the Proprietors Office and dated the 11 day of
December 1747 and bounded Begining at one old Corner white oak on Negro Run and
runing thence North to a white oak on a hill side in an old line of marked trees thence
with line of marked trees to the begining . . . .
Presence of JACOB COONES,   John X Butten
        JOHN COONES
  At a Court held for Culpeper County the 15th of Feby 1779
This Indenture ordered to be recorded.

pp.   On margin: D. D. to JNO. COONES 84
160-   THIS INDENTURE made the 31st day of January 1779 Betwen JOHN BOYER of the
161   state of NORTH CAROLINA of one part and JOHN COONES of the County of Culpe-
        per and State of Virginia of other part Witnesseth that the said John Boyer for
the sum Two hundred and fifty pounds current money of Virginia have granted unto
the said John Coones his heirs for ever land in County of Culpeper granted by Patent
unto WILLIAM HARRIS and from him conveyed unto John Boyer and from him to John
Boyer Son and Heir at Law of the above named John Boyer begining at a pine Corner to
TILMAN WEAVER South to a red oak saplin in a ROAD thence North on a line to JOHN
BUTTEN to two pines thence with a line of SAMUEL PORTERs to three pine Corners
thence with Porters line to one pine Corner to Tilman Weaver on a hill to the begining
containing Two hundred acres of land . . . .
Presence of JACOB COONES,   John Boyer
        JAMES JETT, WILLIAM X BUTTON
  At a Court held for Culpeper County the 15th of Feby 1779
This Indenture with Receipt ordered to be recorded.

p.   On margin: D D to WILLIAM McQUEEN August 1780
162   THIS INDENTURE made the 15th day of February 1779 Betwen ALEXANDER
        McQUEEN of the County of Culpeper of one part and WILLIAM McQUEEN of the
same County Witnesseth that the said Alexander McQueen for good causes but more for
the natual love which he do bear towards his Brother William and the sum of Five Shillings hath granted unto the said William McQueen his heirs land in Culpeper in the
Great Fork of Rappahannock River containing Two hundred acres of land and is
bounded begining at three white oaks thence North thence South to a red oak saplin in
said TUTTs line thence South to the begining said Alexander McQueen hath set his hand
and fixed his Seal the day and year above written.
                                                          Alexander McQueen
  At a Court held for Culpeper County the 15th of February 1779
This Indented Deed of Gift ordered to be recorded.

pp.   On margin: D. D. FRAS. NALLE 1788
162-   THIS INDENTURE made the Eighth day of ( ) in the year 1779 Betwen WILLIAM
165   BROWN Gent of County of Culpeper of one part and MARTIN NALLE JUR. Son of
        JOHN NALLE of the County aforesaid Witnesseth that said William Brown for sum
One hundred and Eleven pounds Current money of Virginia doth grant unto said Mar-

tain Nalle his heirs seventy four acres of land in Culpeper County and Bromfield Parish
in the Great Fork of Rappahannock River lying on both sides Devils Run and bounded
Begining at three pines in a glade side of Devils Run and thence South to two red oak
saplins Corner to THOMAS GRIFFIN thence with another of his lines North to a Hickory
on a ridge in said Martin Nalls line thence with his line South to three red oak saplins
in an Old Mill Pond Corner to said Martain Nalle and JOHN NALLE thence with John Nalls
line to the begining place . . . .
Presence WILLIAM C. BROWN,   William Brown
         THOMAS BROWN, FRANCIS NALLE
   At a Court held for Culpeper County the 15th of Feby 1779
This Indenture (with Memorandum and Receipt) ordered to be recorded.

pp.   On margin: D D to CADR. SLAUGHTER May 1782
165-   TO ALL PEOPLE to whom these presents may come I JOHN SLAUGHTER of County
166   of Culpeper and Parish of Bromfield send Greeting. Know ye that for good
         causes but especially for the love I bear unto my Eldest Son CADWALLADER
SLAUGHTER and for his better suport I have granted unto my abovesaid Son Cadwallader
Slaughter One hundred and forty acres of land in Culpeper County and Bromfield
Parish on the head Branchs of Black Water Run being part of a Track of Five hundred
and forty eight acres of land purchased by said John Slaughter of COL. WILLIAM
CHAMPE and said land is bounded Begining at a red oak Corner to THOMAS YATES in line
of said John Slaughter and BENJAMAN GAINS and runs thence with that line South to a
red oak on the ROAD side leaving the said line runs South to two white oaks on a hill
side near a large Branch and in the line of the said John Slaughter thence North to a
Stoney point a Corner to Thomas Yates thence with his line North to the begining place.
In Witness I have set my hand and fixed my seal the fifteenth day of Feby in year 1779.
                                                                   John Slaughter
   At a Court held for Culpeper County the 15th Feby 1779
This Indenture ordered to be recorded.

pp.   THIS INDENTURE made this 15th of February 1779 Betwen MATTHIS BROYLE and
166-   EVE his Wife of County of Culpeper of one part and GABRIEL LONG of County
168   aforesaid Witnesseth that said Matthias Broyle and Eve his Wife for sum of
         Seven hundred & thirty pounds current money have granted unto the said
Gabriel Long his heirs land in the County aforesaid in the Robinson Fork on the
Branches of Dark Run containing Two hundred and thirty five acres being a track of
land purchased by the said Matthias Broyle of ADAM BROYLE and MARY his Wife by
Deed dated the 15th day of February 1773 recorded in the County Court of Culpeper Be-
gining at three pines Corner to HUNTERS, WILHOIT and MICHAEL BROYLE and North to
two red oaks Corner to said Wilhoit and JOHN WAYLAND and North to one red oak Corner
to JOHN YEGGER and South down the said Branch to Hunters line a pine in the said
Branch and West with Hunters line to the begining. Witness whereof said Matthias
Broile and Eve his Wife have set their Hands and Seals . . . .
                                                                   Matthias Bryle
   At a Court held for Culpeper County the 15th of February   Eve Bryle
1779 This Indenture was ordered to be Recorded. The said
Eve was first privily examined as the Law directs.

pp.   THIS INDENTURE made this 15th of February 1779 Betwen JACOB CHRIMM and
168-   MARGRET his Wife of County of Culpeper of one part and JAMES JONES of said
170   County Witnesseth that said Jacob Chrimm and Margret his Wife for sum of

Two hundred and twenty five pounds current money of Virginia hath sold unto the said
JAMES JONES land in County of Culpeper containing One hundred and twenty acres
being part of a track of Four hundred acres granted to HENRY TYLER of STAFFORD
COUNTY by the right honourable THOMAS LORD FAIRFAX as by Patent from the Pro-
prietors Office dated the 18th day of February 1748 and by the said Henry Tyler sold to
JOHN YANCEY of Culpeper County which was sold by the said John Yancey to said Jacob
Chrimm and bounded begining at three White oaks on the bank of the North side of the
North Branch of the Rush River and runing thence North to a red oak on the side of the
PEAKED MOUNTAIN thence North to a Maple on the bank of the North Branch of the
aforesaid Rush River thence down the meanders of the branch to the begining . . . .
In Presence of GEORGE CALVERT JUNOR,   Jacob Chrimm
        PHILIP GATEWOOD, NATHAN NALLEY   Margrett X Crimm
   At a Court held for Culpeper County the 15th of February 1779
This Indenture from JACOB CRIM and MARGRETT his Wife ordered to be recorded, Pre-
vious to which the said Margrett was first privily examined according to Law.

pp.   THIS INDENTURE made this 19th of April 1777 Betwen JOHN CLORE of County of
170-   Culpeper and KATHRINE his Wife of one part and JOHN CLORE JUNR. of aforesaid
172   County Witnesseth that for sum of Five pounds current money of Virginia the
         said John Clore and Kathrine his Wife do by these presents sell unto the said
John Clore junior his heirs forever One hundred acres of land in the County aforesaid
on the East side of the Robinson River in the ROAD that leads from the DOUBLE TOP
MOUNTAIN thence North to a Chesnut in the said John Clores line thence with his line
to an ash on the said River thence down the courses of said river to the begining . . . .
Presents of WILLIAM GRAYSON,   John Clore
        GEORGE HUME, CHRISTOPHER X CREGLER
   At a Court held for Culpeper County the 15th of March 1779
This Indenture (with Memorandum and Receipt) ordered to be recorded.

pp.   TO ALL PEOPLE to whom these presents shall come Know ye that I JOHN CLORE of
172-   County of Culpeper and Parish of Bromfield for the love I do bear to my Son
173   MICHAEL CLORE of the same County and Parish do grant to my said Son Michael
         Clore One hundred acres of land in the same County and Parish being part of the
track of land I now live including the Plantation whereon said Michel now lives
bounded as nearly in a Squear as the lines of his Brother JOHN CLORE and my own lines
will admit if his house and Plantation being included in the said One hundred acres.
Witness my hand and seal this thirty first day of December 1776.
Presents of GEORGE WETHERALL,   John Clore
        GEORGE WILHOIT, WM. CHAMPMAN,
        BENJAMIN ZACHARY
   At a Court held for Culpeper County the 15th of March 1779
This Indenture Deed of Gift ordered to be recorded.

pp.   On margin: D D to Self 84
173-   TO ALL PEOPLE Know ye that I JAMES WHITE of the County of Culpeper and
174   Parish of Bromfield for good causes as well as for the Natual love I do bear to my
         beloved Son ARMISTEAD WHITE (the hereafter reserves being first and Amply
complied with) do give him the said Armistead all my Estate both real and personal to
him forever he paying to my Son ABBOTT WHITE one hundred pound at my decease and
to my Grand Daughter LUCEY CAMPBELL one hundred pound at my Decease and makes a
good right to MARGARET GAINS my Grand Daughter in one Negroe wench named Mille

and her increase now in the actual possession of my Son in Law JAMES GAINS who is to have the said Negroe till my Grand Daughter arrives to Lawfull age or Maries and shall in the time of my own and my Wife MAGARETs life suppourt and maintain us his Father and Mother and my Grand Children Margaret Gains and Lucey Campbell till they shall come to Lawfull Age or Marries in a reasonable manner suitable to the Estate he now takes possession of but in case he fails to do and perform his part of the support and Maintenance to either of the above mentioned four persons that then the whole Estate to be as this Deed of Gift had never been Wrote but in case he should perform his part then he is to have all my Estate from the date hereof. In Witness whereof I have set my hand and Seal this 4 day of Octor. 1778.

Presents of GEORGE WETHERALL,   James X White
     ROBERT SHOTWELL, HANNAH SHOTWELL,
     ANN WETHERALL, MARY WETHERALL
  At a Court held for Culpeper County the 15th of March 1779
This Indented Deed of Gift ordered to be recorded.

pp.   THIS INDENTURE made this day of in the year 1778 Betwen ADAM CLORE and
174-   MARGRET his Wife of the County of Culpeper of one part and PAUL LEATHER of
176   aforesaid County Witnesseth that for the sum Six pounds current money of Vir-
        ginia said Adam Clore and Margret his Wife have sold unto the said Paul Leather
his heirs forever Thirteen acres of land in the County of Culpeper and bounded Begining at a white oak on the South side of a Branch Corner of said Clores thence with
another line North to a gum in said Paul Leathers Plantation thence with another of
Line of Clores South to the Begining . . . .
Presents of JOSHUA LEATHER,   Adam Clore
     NICHLES LEATHER, SAMUEL LEATHER   Margret X Clore
  At a Court held for Culpeper County the 15th day of March 1779
This Indenture ordered to be recorded.

pp.   On margin: D D to JAS QUINN 28th June 84
176-   THIS INDENTURE made the Twenty Ninth day of January 1779 Between JOHN
178   ROGERS of Culpeper County and TABBATHA his Wife of one part and JAMES
        QUINN of Culpeper County of other part Witnesseth that John Rogers and Tab-
batha his Wife for sum of One hundred pounds current money of Virginia hath granted
unto the said James Quinn his heirs forever land in the Parish of Bromfield and County
of Culpeper containing Three hundred acres bounded Begining at three pines in
CHARLES BLUNTs line runing South to three pines on a hill corner a small distance
from Stony Branch thence East to two pines a new corner made Betwen John Rogers
and Charles Blunt thence with said Blunts line South to the begining . . . .
                                  John Rogers
  At a Court held for Culpeper County the 15th of March 1779   Tabitha Rogers
This Indenture ordered to be recorded previous to which the
said Tabitha was first privily examined according to Law.

pp.   THIS INDENTURE made the 15th day of February 1779 Betwen JACOB CRIM and
178-   ANNE his Wife of County of Culpeper of one part and JAMES SIMS of the County
180   aforesaid Witnesseth that the said Jacob Crim and Anne his Wife for sum of
        seventy pounds current money of Virginia do grant unto the said James Sims his
heirs One hundred and three acres of land in Culpeper County and Bromfield Parish in
the Great Fork of Rappahanock bounded Begining at two red oaks a Corner to MARTIN
NALLE JUNOR in the said THOMAS GRIFINs line and runs thence North thence East to

three pines a Corner to CAPT. JOHN TUTT thence North to a Hikory in the line of Martin
Nalle Junr. thence with his lines South to the begining place . . . .
Presents of us WILLIAM BEAZLEY

Jacob Crim junr.
Anne Crim

At a Court held for Culpeper County the 15th of March 1779
This Indenture (with Memorandum and Receipt) ordered to be recorded the said Anne
being first privily examined according to Law.

pp.   On margin: D. D. to JNO. GIBBS 29th Jany 1781
180-   THIS INDENTURE made this Thirteenth day of August 1778 Betwen RICHARD
183.   BOHANNON and BETTY his Wife of Parish of Bromfield in Culpeper County of one
         part and JOHN GIBBS of Parish and County aforesaid Witnesseth that said Richard
Bohannon and Betty his Wife for sum of Four hundred and Eleaven pounds current
money of Virginia doth grant to the said John Gibbs his heirs forever land in the
Parish and County aforesaid containing Two hundred and thirty five acres it being the
land that ELIOT BOHANNON SER. his Father gave to his Son Richard Bohannon on
records of said County by a Deed bounded Begining at two Pines North thence South
West to a red oak North to a branch West to a large white oak in MARTIN ROSEs line
North to a red oak Corner in said Roses line South to one hicory on the head of a branch
thence down the Branch to the begining . . . .
Presents of JOSEPH WOOD,   Richard Bohannon
     JAMES BARBOUR, ALEXANDER WAUGH,   Betty Bohannon
     JOSEPH WOOD, ZACHARIAH GIBBS,
     FRANCIS MADISON
 The Commonwealth of Virginia Whereas Richard Bohannon and Betty his Wife have
sold land in the County aforesaid and said Betty cannot travil to our Court of Culpeper to
make acknowledgement of the said conveyance we do command you to go to the said
Betty and examine her and when you have received her acknowledgement that you
Certify us thereof in our Court. Witness JOHN JAMESON Clk of our Court this day of 1778.
 Persuant to the within Commission we did personally go to the said Betty Bohannon
and examine her apart from her husband touching the acknowledgement of the said
conveyance and she declared she did the same freely and willing should be recorded in
Court of Culpeper this 14 day of August 1778.
                              JOSEPH WOOD   JAMES BARBOUR
At a Court held for Culpeper County the 15th of March 1779
This Indenture with Commisheon thereon annexed & Cerrtified is ordered to be
recorded.

pp.   On margin: D. D. to JNO. SAMPSON 1786
183-   THIS INDENTURE made this 19th day of October 1778 Betwen RICHARD HAMTON
185   of County of Culpeper and SUSANNAH his Wife of one part and BENJAMIN FIN-
         NELL of said County Witnesseth that the said Richard Hamton and Susannah his
Wife for sum of Three hundred and Sixty eight pounds current money have sold unto
Benjamin Finnill his heirs forever Three hundred and sixty eight acres bounded begining at four small white oaks on a ridge on the South of the PEIRSONS ROAD thence
South to three pines on a ridge Corner to ROBERT MEDLEY thence with his line South to
three small oaks in MAY BURTONs line near a small Plantation of JOHN BARNETTs
thence with his line North to three white oaks on the North side of a Branch of
GRYMESES RUN Corner to the said Burton thence with his line North to a white oak

Corner to JACOB MEDLEY and JOHN TERRILL on a small Branch thence with Terrills line cross the LOST MOUNTAIN North to a large pine about ten poles from a Branch Corner to said Terrill thence North to the begining . . . .

Presence of JOSEPH WOOD,   Richard Hampton
      ROBERT ALCOCK, ZACHARIAS GIBBS,   Susanna Hampton
      FRANCIS GIBBS, JOSEPH WOOD JUNIOR

  The Commonwealth of Virginia to JOSEPH WOOD and ROBERT ALCOCK Gent. Whereas Richard Hampton and Susanna his Wife have sold to Benjamin Finnell land in the County of Culpeper and Whereas the said Susanna cannot travel to our Court to make acknowledgement of the said conveyance we give you power to go to the said Susanna and examine her privily and when you have received her acknowledgement that you Certify us thereof in our said Court. Witness JOHN JAMESON Clk of our Court the 5 day of November in the third year of the Commonwealth.

  Pursuant to a Commission we Joseph Wood and Robt. Alcock two of the Commissioners therein mentioned went to Susanna Hampton who acknowledged the same in our presents privately and apart from her Husband that she was willing same be recorded this fifth day of November 1778.   JOSEPH WOOD   ROBERT ALCOCK

  At a Court held for Culpeper County the 19th of October 1778

This Indenture ordered to be recorded with the Dedimus & Certificate thereto annexed.

p.   THIS INDENTURE made this 12th day February 1779 Betwen WILLIAM FIELD and
186   HANNAH his Wife of one part and BENJAMIN FIELD of other part Witnesseth that
       for the sum of Six hundred pounds Lawfull money but more for the Love and affection we have for our Beloved Son hath granted unto the said Benjamin his heirs forever land in the County of Culpeper on the East side of Flatt Run and bounded Begining on Flatt Run at a walnut standing near the bank of the run and runeth thence North East and thence to NORMANS FORD OLD ROAD reserving four acres three roods and thirty two chain according to a survey made by Mr. JOHN TRIPLETT Betwen the above-mentioned and SKREENs line and thence runing along the said old road the several courses thereof a white oak standing on the North side of said Road reserving Sixteen acres betwen the said old road and Skreens line agreeable to a Servey made by JOHN HUME Oct the 5, 1770 and on the Platt father reference may be had and from the above mentioned white oak the lines runs South to a forked ash standing on the Bank of Flatt Run thence up the said Run as it meanders to the begining the said Bound containing Two hundred and twenty three acres according to CAPT JOHN TRIPLETTs Platt . . . .

Presents of ARGYLE TAYLOR,   Wm. Field
      GEORGE ASHBY, FAUSHEE TEBBS,   Hannah Field
      JOHN PAYTON

  At a Court held for Culpeper County the 15th of March 1779

This Indenture Deed of Gift ordered to be recorded previous to which the sd Hannah was first privily examined according to Law.

p.   On margin: D. D. Octr. 3, 1780
187   KNOW ALL MEN to whom these presents shall come that I CHARLES THORNTON of
       the County of Essix do sell unto WILLIAM HUGHES of the County of Culpeper three negroes Vizt. Sarah, James and Charles upon this Condition that is said Wm. Hughs do pay unto said Charles Thornton eight hundred pounds in April seventy nine and said Thorton is warrant the said negroes but in case the said Hughs do not pay the money according to the time appointed said Thornton shall have a right to the Neagroes or Twelve hundred pound like money this 17th of December 1778.

Test DENNIS CROW,   Charles Thornton
    ELIZABETH GAINS
 Freds: 10th March 1779 Recd. of Mr. Wm. Hughes Eight hundred pounds in full of the
within Bill of Sale for which have sign'd Duplicate receipt of same Tennes and date for
Charles Thornton.
Test JOHN HUGHES, DENNIS CROW   . JAMES HUNTER
  At a Court held for Culpeper County the 15th of March 1779
This Bill of Sale ordered to be recorded.

pp.   On margin: D D ABEL JANNY 1794
187-   THIS INDENTURE made the 15th day of March 1779 Between FREDERICK ZIMMER-
189   MAN and SARAH his Wife of County of Culpeper of one part and RUBIN ZIM-
       MERMAN his Son of said County of other part Witnesseth that said Frederick
Zimmerman and Sarah his Wife for Six hundred pounds current money of Virginia
hath granted unto the said Reuben Zimmerman land in the County of Culpeper being
part of a tract commonly call'd MOUNT PONEY containing One hundred and twenty
acres bounded begining at two white oaks in CARTERs old line thence with that line
South to two red oak saplins North to two small Maples in a branch in line of JOHNSON's
lott thence with his line South to a white oak stump in Zimmermans old lott line thence
South to the begining . . . .
Presents of WILLIAM ALLAN,   Frederick Zimmerman
    G. TRIPLETT, ROBERT WRIGHT   Sarah Zimmerman
  At a Court held for Culpeper County the 15th of March 1779
This Indenture of Bargain and Sale ordered to be recorded Previous to which the said
Sarah was first previly examined according to Law.

pp.   THIS INDENTURE made this 21st day of December 1778 Betwen CHARLES PAYTON
189-   of County of Culpeper and SARAH his Wife of one part and ISRAEL ROBERTSON
190   of County of STAFFORD of other part Witnesseth that for sum of Three hundred &
       seven pounds current money of Virginia the said Charles Payton and Sarah his
Wife have sold unto the said Israel Robertson eighty five acres of land in the aforesaid
County and bounded Begining at a Maple standing upon the North side of Mountain Run
runing thence North to two Maples at a Spring thence North to a white oak standing on
the bank of the run thence down the run to the Begining . . . .
Presents of us BENJAMIN ROBERTS,   Charles Payton
    RICHARD BANKS, THOMAS BROWN   Sarah Payton
  At a Court held for Culpeper County the 15th of March 1779
  This Indenture ordered to be recorded Previous to which the said Sarah was first
privily examined according to Law.

pp.   On margin: D D yr Ord 1794
191-   THIS INDENTURE made this fifteenth day of March 1779 Between ALEXANDER
193   BAXTER and MARY his Wife of the County of Culpeper of one part and GEORGE
       CALVERT JUNR. of said County Witnesseth that said Alexander Baxter and Mary
his Wife for sum of Seventy five pounds current money of Virginia have granted unto
said George Calvert junr. his heirs forever One hundred acres of land bounded
begining at a white oak thence South to the begining and bounded likewise on every
line by the said George Calvert junr. . . . . .
Presence of DAVID BAKER,   Alexander Baxter
    CHARLES STEWARD, WILLIAM DUNCAN Y   Mary ⨍B Baxter

At a Court held for Culpeper County the 15th of Mary 1779
This Indenture ordered to be recorded Previous to which the said Mary was first privily
examined as the Law directs.

pp.   On margin: D D Augt 1786
193-   THIS INDENTURE made this XIXth day of March 1779 Betwen FRANCIS WAIN-
195   WRIGHT LEA and MARY his Wife of County of Culpeper of one part and LEAWIS
         CONNER of County of Culpeper of other part Witnesseth that said Francis Wain-
wright Lea and Mary his Wife for the sum Five hundred pounds current money of Virginia hath granted unto said LEWIS CONNER his heirs two tracts of land containing One
hundred and fifty three acres with the Mill tu the same in the County aforesaid Rela-
tion being thereunto had bounded Begining at a hickory on a rock on the North side of
the Robinson River opposit the Mill and runing thence North to a Locust in the field
thence North to a red oak in the old line, thence with the said line North to a parcel of
Maples in Bever Dam Run thence down the said run to a hickory on the said run at the
mouth of the said run the bank of the river thence up the river to the begining containing One hundred and seventy six acres Also the other part being on the South side
of the Robinson River begining at three white oaks on the bank of the river above the
Hill thence South to some stones on the bank of Holems Run thence up the several
courses of the said run to a white oak on the said run thence leaving the run and
runing with the Deviding line Betwen the said Wainwright Lea and BENJAMIN PETTY
North to a Gum on the river thence up the several courses of the River to the begining
containing Twenty seven acres . . . .

                                                              Francis Wainwright Lea
At a Court held for Culpeper County the 15th March 1779   Mary Lea
This Indenture ordered to be recorded Previous to which the sd
Mary was first privily examined as the Law directs.

pp.   On margin: D D 1791
195-   THIS INDENTURE made the 15th of March 1779 Betwen WILLIAM ROBERTS of
197   Culpeper County Surviving and Acting Executor and SARAH CORBIN Executrix
         of the Last Will and Testament of WILLIAM JOHNSON deceased of one part and
WILLIAM HUGHES of the County aforesaid Witnesseth that the said William Roberts and
Sarah Corbin persuant and according to the Last Will of the aforesaid William Johnston
deceast which is in records of Culpeper County Court impowering them to do the same
and for consideration of One hundred and fourteen pounds 5/ current money of Virginia for the Benefit of the said Deceased Estate and Orpans do grant unto the aforesaid
William Hughes his heirs Fifty two and one half acre in County of Culpeper County and
Bromfield Parish in the Little Fork of Rappahannock River joining on Battle Run and
bounded Begining at a forked Spanish oak on the bank of Battle Run on the East side
thereof and runs North to the begining place . . . .
Presence of JOHN C. COCKE,   William Roberts
    JOHN STROTHER, JOHN STROTHER ,   Sarah Corbin
    JOHN STROTHER JUNR.
At a Court held for Culpeper County the 15th day of March 1779
This Indenture was acknowledged by Wm. Roberts & ordered to be recorded as to him,
and at a Court held for the said County the 17th day of February 1780 was partly proved
as to Sarah Corbin, by one of the Witnesses thereto & ordered to be Certified as to her,
and at a Court held for the said County the 18th of September 1780, This Indenture was
further proved as to Sarah Corbin by John Strother & ordered to be certified.

pp.   On margin: D. D., 1795
198-   THIS INDENTURE made the 15th of March 1799 Betwen RICHARD PARKS and
199   MARY his Wife of the County of Culpeper of one part and WILLIAM PURVIS of
         County aforesaid Witnesseth that said Richard Parks and Mary his Wife for the
sum Thirty two pound current money of Virginia have granted unto the said William
Purvis his heirs land containing Fifty nine acres in Culpeper County and Bromfield
Parish in the Gourd Vine Fork of Rappahannock River lying and joining on Black
Water Run and Jonathans Run the same being part of Seven hundred acres of land said
Richard Parks now lives on and the Fifty nine acres is bounded Begining at three white
oaks on Black Water Run Corner to Richard Parks and Corner to a servey of said William
Purvis thence with Parks old line crossing the said Run thence South to three pines
Corner to said Purvis's late Servey and WILLIAM DUNCANs thence with the said line to
the Begining . . . .
                                                                    Richard Parks

   At a Court held for Culpeper County the 15th of March 1779
This Indenture ordered to be recorded.

pp.   On margin; D D CHAPMAN Augt 18th. 83
200-   THIS INDENTURE made this 24 day of February 1779 Betwen JOHN ROOTES of
201   GLOUCESTER COUNTY of one part and WILLIAM CHAMPMAN of Culpeper County
         Witnesseth that for sum of Fifty pounds current money of Virginia to him paid
the said John Rootes have sold unto sd William Champman his heirs forever Two hundred and twenty acres of land Begining at two poplars Corner trees to a patten formely
granted to WILLIAM RUSH now Champmans thence runing with his line South to two
chesnuts a Corner in another line formely granted to THOMAS PHILLIPS now CHRISTO-
PHERS thence with his line West to a Chesnut by a Great Rock a Corner to Christopher
formerly Rootes thence leaving his line to a Spanish oak on the South side of a ridge of
the DOUBLE TOP MOUNTAIN thence North to the begining . . . .
Presence of GEORGE HUME,   John Rootes
         FRANCIS TURNLEY, THOMAS CHAMPMAN
   At a Court held for Culpeper County the 15th day of March 1779
This Indenture ordered to be recorded.

pp.   On margin: D D Self 1801
201-   THIS INDENTURE made this Twenty second day of February 1779 Betwen ROBERT
203   EASTHAM SENIOR of County of Culpeper and ANNE his Wife of one part and
         ROBERT FREEMAN JUNOR of the same County Witnesseth that said Robert Eastham
senior for the sum One hundred & fifty pounds current money of Virginia have
granted unto said Robert Freeman land in the Great Fork of the County of Culpeper
known by the name of CUBY containing One hundred and ninety four acres bounded
begining at a white oak near a pond Corner to WILLIAM STEWARD and runing with his
line West to a Corner of CHRISTOPHER HOOMES thence with said Hoomes line South to the
begining . . . .
Presence of JAMES PENDLETON,   Robt. Eastham
         FRANCIS MORGAN, JOHN SLAUGHTER,   Ann Eastheim
         JOHN DILLARD JUNR.
   Culpeper County SC The Commonwealth sends Greeting to JOHN SLAUGHTER, JAMES
PENDLETON and ROBERT EASTHAM Gent Whereas Robert Eastham and Ann his Wife have
sold unto Robert Freeman junr. land in the County and whereas the said Ann is unable
to travel to our Court aforesaid to make acknowledgement of the said conveyance we
therefore relying on your providentian & Circumspection require you to cause the said

Ann to come before you & examine her apart from her sd Husband touching her acknowledgement of the said Indenture and having there obtained her acknowledged Certify our Justices thereof in our Court. Witness JOHN JAMESON Clk of our Court this 22nd
of February 1779 in the Fourth year of the Commonwealth.

Culpeper Sct We the Subscribers in obedience to the within writ have cause the within named Eastham to come before us and examined her touching her acknowledgement freely acknowledged the same and desires same should be recorded in the Court of
Culpeper. In Witness this 22nd day of February 1779.

                         JOHN SLAUGHTER   JAMES PENDLETON
At a Court held for Culpeper County the 15th of March 1779
This Indenture from ROBERT EASTHAM JR. and Ann his Wife ordered to be recorded.

pp.   THIS INDENTURE made the 24th of August 1778 Betwen HUGH FREEMAN and
204-   ANNE his Wife of County of Culpeper of one part and GAVIN LAWSON of same
206   County Witnesseth that ROBERT FREEMAN of said County of Culpeper and Father
         of said Hugh stood seized as tenant in fee Tail of One thousand acres of land on
Mill Run in the said County and by Virtue of an Act of the General Assembly made in
the 22d year of his late Majesty George the second of Great Britain obtained a Writ from
the Secretarys Office in the nature of an ad quod damnun directed to the Sherif of said
County commanding him to enquire by the Oaths of good and lawfull men of his Baili-
wic the value of the said one thousand acres of land with appurtinances and whether
the same be parcel of or contiguous to other entailed lands in the possession and seizen
of said Robert Freeman which said Sherif and Jury did report in their inquision and
return unto said Office the said Lands were of value of one hundred and ninety five
pounds Sterling and were not parcel of or contiguous to other Entailed lands in possession of the said Robert Freeman whereby and by force of the said Act of the General
Assembly said Robert Freeman enabled to sell the said lands to the said Hugh Freeman
and to his heirs forever in fee simple and whereas the said Robert Freeman by Deed of
Gift dated the 13 day of October in the year 1770 recorded in the Court of Culpeper did
for consideration of natural love make over unto said Hugh Freeman and his heirs and
that during the natual life of said Robert Two hundred and thirty acres of land being
part of the track above mentioned and did likewise by a Deed of Bargain and Sale dated
the 20 day of June in the year 1774 convey unto said Hugh for Two hundred pounds all
that tenement situate on the West side of Mill Run being the same whereon the said
Hugh Freeman now lives and supposed to contain Four hundred acres and being part of
the entailed land and which last mentioned Deed recorded in Court of Culpeper NOW
THIS INDENTURE WITNESSETH that the said Hugh Freeman and Ann his Wife for sum of
Seven hundred & fifty pounds current money paid sell unto said Gavin Lawson his
heirs all that land in County of Culpeper now in the possession of the said Hugh Freeman and his tenents and granted to him in manner aforesaid by the said Robert Freeman and which he obliges himself and does contain five hundred acres at the least and
Bounded Begining at the mouth of Mill Run and from thence up the Elk or Easthams
River to a Locust on the river bank a Corner to JAMES PENDLETON then with another of
his lines North thence to a red oak on the said Mill Run and from thence down the Run
to the Begining To have and To Hold the said Tract of land with the MILL thereon with
the appurtinances unto the sd Gavin Lawson . . . .
Presents of us JOHN WIGGINTON,   Hugh Freeman
        HANCOCK LEE, ALEXANDER BRUCE,   Ann Freeman
        JOHN LAWSON, JAMES READ,
        ROBERT FREEMAN, WILLIAM McCLANAHAM

The Commonwealth of Virginia to WILLIAM McCLANAHAM & JOHN WIGGINTON Gent Whereas Hugh Freeman and Anne his Wife have sold unto Gavin Lawson land in the County of Culpeper and Whereas the said Anne cannot travel to our County Court to make acknowledgement of the said conveyance we give you power to go to the said Anne and examine her whether she doth the same freely and when you have received her acknowledgement that you Certifie us thereof in our Court. Witness JOHN JAMESON Clk of our said Court the 25th of August 1778 in the third year of the Commonwealth.

In Consequence of the within Commission we have privily examined the within named Anne Freeman apart from her husband and she acknowledges having freely signed the Deed without threats of her husband and is willing the same be recorded. In Witness this 14th day of December 1778.

WILLIAM McCLANAHAN   JOHN WIGGINTON

At a Court held for Culpeper County the 15th day of March 1779
This Indenture with a Commission & Certificate thereon is ordered to be recorded.

pp. 206-207
THIS INDENTURE made this 15th of May 1779 Between THOMAS and MARY ANN his Wife of the County of Culpeper of one part and JASON THOMAS of the County aforesaid Witnesseth that THOMAS PRATT and MARY ANN his Wife for the sum of Twenty pounds current money of Virginia have granted unto the said Jason Thomas his heirs Four hundred and forty acres of land in County of Culpeper bounded Begining at a red & white oak Corner to Mr. NICHOLAS BATTAILE and SAMUEL KENNELEY thence with the said Kenneleys line East to white oaks in the said KENNERLEYs line on the South side of a Mountain and some Branches in a line of THOMAS KENNERLEYs thence with his line North to a white oak Corner of said Kennerleys thence leaving said Kennerleys line thence to a white oak on the side of a mountain thence South to a Dogwood in a small branch Corner to said Nicholas Battailie thence with his line South to the begining . . . .

Thomas Pratt
Maryann Pratt

At a Court held for Culpeper County the 15th of March 1779
This Indenture ordered to be recorded Previous to which the said Mary Ann was first privily examined according to Law.

pp. 207-209
On margin: D. D. to WM. ROBERTS
THIS INDENTURE made the 15th day of May 1779 Betwen THOMAS PRAT of County of Culpeper of one part and JOHN FLINT of County of Culpeper of other part Witnesseth that for sum of Sixty pounds Current money of Virginia the said Thomas Pratt and MARY ANN his Wife hath granted unto the said John Flint his heirs forever land in the County of Culpeper containing Two hundred and forty two acres bounded Begining at a pine Corner RICHARD FLINT JUNR. No. West to a red oak in a line of CHRISTIAN RYNERs thence South to a box Oak in a Branch Corner to said Riner & SAMUEL CARSEY thence South to a large white oak on a Branch Corner to CROSSWIT thence South East to the begining . . . .

Thomas Pratt
Mary Ann Pratt

At a Court held for Culpeper County the 15th of March 1779
This Indenture ordered to be recorded the said Mary Ann being first privily examined according to Law.

pp. 209-210
THIS INDENTURE made the 22nd day of February 1779 Betwen GEORGE CUN-NEARD of the County of Culpeper and ELIZABETH his Wife of one part and HENRY FIELD of the aforesaid County Witnesseth that for the sum of Two hundred and fifty pounds current money of Virginia the said George KINNAIRD and his Wife

Elizabeth whereof they do sell unto the said Henry Field his heirs forever One hundred and twenty five acres of land in the aforesaid County and bound begining at a Box Oak by the ROAD side and two Spanish Oaks by said road that is called FINLASONS ROAD thence North to a Poplar upon the side of a Branch thence North to 2 spanish Oaks upon a ridge thence North to a red oak in one old line thence South to the begining containing One hundred and twenty five acres of land . . . .

Presence of WILLIAM BALL,   George Kinnaird
    JOHN WALLIS, LEONAR BARNS   Elizabeth Kinnaird
  At a Court held for Culpeper County the 15th of March 1779
This Indenture ordered to be recorded.

pp.   On margin: D D 1789
211-   THIS INDENTURE made this 23rd day of October 1778 Betwen GEORGE CALVERT
214   and LYDIA his Wife of County of Culpeper and Colony of Virginia of one part
         and JOHN CALVERT of BALTIMORE COUNTY and Colony of MARYLAND Witnsseth
that the said George Calvert Junr. and Lydia his Wife for the sum Four hundred and thirty five pounds current money of Virginia paid by the said John Calvert he the said George Calvert junr. and Lydia his Wife do grant unto the said John Calvert his heirs land in the County of Culpeper (it being part of a large tract of 1931 acres granted to JOHN FROGG and MICHAEL WALLACE by Patent Bearing date the 27th of June 17-1 and conveyed to George Calvert junr. by John Frogg by Deeds bearing date the 25 and 26 days of March 1777 containing Eight hundred and twenty six acres of land) bounded Begining at two chesnuts and a spanish Oak Corner to CAPT. McCLANAHANs line South to a small box oak thence leaving McClanahans line and with the Patent line thence South leaving the Patent line to a small chesnut tree on the side of a Mountain thence North East to 3 hikories near NIX'S ARM thence South leaving the Patent line to the begining . . . .

Presence of JOHN BRADFORD,   George Calvert junr.
    JAMES BROWNING, THOMAS McCLANAHAN,   Lydia B. Calvert
    JOHN STROTHER, JOHN SLAUGHTER
  Provided always and it is my intent that the above mentioned John Calvert his heirs nor assigns shall not molest nor disturbe my Father GEORGE CALVERT SENR. during his natual life but suffer him Peacibly to ocupy and enjoy Two hundred and fifty acres of land whereon he now lives it being part of the above mentioned land and Binding on the Patent line above the HORSE SHOE and on the South side of the said line of Division to proceed from three red oaks standing near a branch near the place where BEN SMOOT lived and Corner to the Patent to the intent that my Father may possess the said Two hundred and fifty acres of land during his natual life and no longer . . . .
                                                        George Calvert junr.
  The Commonwealth of Virginia to JOHN STROTHER, JOHN SLAUGHTER and WILLIAM BROWN Greeting Whereas George Calvert and Lydia his Wife have sold unto John Calvert land in Culpeper County and whereas the said Lydia cannot travil to our County Court of Culpeper to make acknowledgement of the said conveyance we do give you power to receive her acknowledgement of said conveyance and when you have received her acknowledgement that you Certify us thereof in our said Court. Witness JOHN JAMESON Clk of our said Court at the house aforesaid the 24th day of October 1778.
  Culpeper SCT By Virtue of the within Writ we caused the within named Lydia Calvert to come before us and examined her apart from her husband Touching her acknowledgement of the Deed who freely acknowedged the same. In Witness this first day of March 1779.
                        JOHN STROTHER   JOHN SLAUGHTER

At a Court held for Culpeper County the 15th of March 1779
This Indenture with the Commission annexed and the Certificate thereon is ordered to
be recorded.

pp.   On margin: D D PH. SLAUGHTER p order 1798
214-   This Indenture made the 15th day of March 1779 Betwen BENJAMIN LILLARD
216   and FRANKY his Wife of the County of Culpeper of one part and PAUL LEATHER
         of County aforesaid Witnesseth that the said Benjamin Lillard and Frankey his
Wife for the sum Two hundred and Fifty pounds current money of Virginia have
granted unto the said Paul Leather his heirs One hundred and sixty one acres of land in
the County of Culpeper and is bounded Begining at two chesnut oaks on the side of the
LONG MOUNTAIN thence North to a three pronged Chusnut Corner to SAMUEL LEATHER
thence with his line to LEWIS RENDERs line thence to JAMES YOWELLs line thence with
his line the several courses to the top of a Mountain at DAVID YOWELLS ROAD there to
the Begining it being all the land belonging to the said Benjamin Lillard where he now
lives . . . .

Benjamin Lillard
Frankey Lillard

     The Commonwealth of Virginia to WM. BROWN, JOHN SLAUGHTER and GEORGE
WEATHERALL Gent Whereas Benjamin Lillard and Frankey his Wife have sold unto Paul
Leather land in County of Culpeper and Whereas the said Frankey cannot travel to our
Court of Culpeper to make acknowledgement of the said conveyance we give you power
to go to the said Frankey and receive her acknowledgement of same apart from her
husband and when you have recd. her acknowledgement that you Certifie us thereof in
our said Court. Witness JOHN JAMESON Clk of our Court the 23rd day of August 1779 in
the third year of the Commonwealth.
     By Virtue of the within Commission to us the Subscribers we did go to the said Frankey
and her did examine apart from her husband and she freely acknowledged that she did
desire the Deed should be recorded in the Court of Culpeper. In Witness this 23rd day of
August 1779.

WM. BROWN   JOHN SLAUGHTER

     At a Court held for Culpeper County the 15th of March 1779
This Indenture ordered to be recorded and on the motion of the said Paul Leather a
Commission is awarded to take the private Examination of the said Frankey which when
returned is with the Certificate thereon ordered to be recorded.

pp: THIS INDENTURE made this 12 October 1769 Between WILLIAM TWYMAN of Cul-
216-   peper County of one part and ADAM GARR of the above County of other part
217   Witnesseth that William Twyman for the sum of Eleaven pounds four shillings
         current money granted unto the said Adam Garr his heirs forever Thirty acres
of land in the abovesaid County and joining the said Garr and bounded begining at a
white oak an LOOKs thence South to two pines near a branch thence to two white oaks
thence East to two pines near a branch thence East to white oak saplins by the COURT
HOUSE ROAD thence South East to a Maple in the Fork of the Run thence up the several
courses of the run to a Double Maple Corner to JOSEPH EARLEY thence South East to
another Corner of the said Earley and Garr thence with Garr line to the begining
Whereof the said William Twyman and WINNEFRED TWYMAN hath set their hands and
seals . . . .
In presents of us JOHN WILSON,   William Twyman
        MICHAEL GARR, JOHN WAYLAND   Winnefred Twyman

At a Court held for Culpeper the 17th of May 1770
This Indenture was proved by the Oath of two of the Witnesses thereto and is ordered to be certified.
    At a Court held for Culpeper County the 15th day of March 1779
This Indenture was acknowledged by the said William Twyman and ordered to be recorded.

pp.   THIS INDENTURE made the 29th day of October in the Year of our Lord 1776 and
217- the FIRST YEAR of the AMERICAN free and Independent States by and Betwen
219   AMBROSE YARBROUGH and MARY his Wife of the County of Culpeper and Parish
      of St. Marks of one part and HENRY LEWIS of the same County and Parish of
Bromfield of other part Witnesseth that said Ambroese Yarbrough and Mary his Wife
for the sum of Fifteen Pounds current money have sold unto the said Henry Lewis land
in the aforesaid County and Parish of Bromfield containing Sixty eight acres which said
land was granted to the said Yarbrough by the right Honourable THOMAS LORD FAIRFAX
by Deed bearing date the Twelth day of December MDXXLIX and is bounded begining at a
large locust in a line of said Henry Lewises on the South side of a branch of the Robinson River and thence runing up the several courses of the said South Fork to 2
hickories in said Branch leaving the river North to a Chesnut Oak on the side of the
DOUBLE TOP MOUNTAIN thence North to a rock in the Fork of a Branch of the said
Robinson River and thence North to the begining . . . .
Presents of us AMBROSE BOHANNON,   Ambrose Yarbrough
    RICHARD DICKEN, HENRY YOWELL,   Mary Yarbrough
    RUBEN MEDLEY
    At a Court held for the County of Culpeper the 15th day of March 1777
This Indenture was proved by the oaths of two of the witnesses thereto which is ordered
to be certified.
    At a Court held for the County of Culpeper the 15th day of March 1779
This Indenture was fully proved by another Witness thereto & ordered to be recorded.

pp.   On margin: D D yr. Ord. 1794
219- THIS INDENTURE TRIPARTITE made this 30th day of May in 1777 Betwen THOMAS
221   LAWSON and JOHN LEE Gent Executors of the Last Will and Testament of ALLAN
      MACRAE Gent Deceased of one part, JOHN FROGG Gent of the second part and
GEORGE CALVERT JUNR. of the County of Culpeper Planter of the Third part. Whereas
the said John Frogg by his Deed of Lease and Release dated the 2d and 3d of May 1759
Morgaged to the said Allan Macrae in his life time among other messuages land in the
County of Culpeper for consideration in said Deed mentioned and Whereas the County
Court of PRINCE WILLIAM upon the 15th day of April 1774 among other things ordered
and decreed that the Sheriff of the said County of Culpeper should after the expiration
of three months from that date sell the then remaining part of the said lands in Cul-
peper County (except a Sale out of the same of One hundred acres made to a Certain
ALEXANDER BAXTER) and pay to the said Executors of Allan Macrae the sum of 242
pounds 12 Shillings with intrest from the second day of September 1773 until paid and
Whereas the said Sheriff of Culpeper exposed the said lands to sale according to the
Decree aforesaid and they were purchased of him by the said George Calvert junr. NOW
THIS INDENTURE WITNESSETH that the said Thomas Lawson and John Lee for the sum of
242 pounds 12 shilings with interest to them according to the Decree aforesaid paid by
the Sheriff of Culpeper Before the ensealing of these presents have with the consent of
the said John Frogg released and Quit claim & by these presents do for themselves and
their Executors and for the heirs of Allan Macrae released unto the said George Calvert

junr. and his heirs all the Estate right which the said Allan Macrae in his lifetime had
and they the said John Lawson and John Lee now have to the said lands . . . .
Presents of us THOMAS McCLANAHAN   )   Thos. Lawson Exr. of
         WILLIAM McCLANAHAN, DANIEL STEWARD)   ·   Mr. Allen Macrae
         ARCHD. BIGBEE   )   Jno. Lee. Exr. of Mr. Macrae
         RICHARD SCOTT, CHARLES STEWARD) Evidences to Lawsons Signing
   At a Court held for Culpeper County the 20th of October 1777
This Indenture Tripartite was proved as to Thomas Lawson and John Frogg by two of the
Witnesses thereto and ordered to be certified as to them, and by three witnesses as to
John Lee & ordered to be recorded as to him.
   At a Court held for the said County the 15th day of March 1779
This said Indenture was fully proved and ordered to be recorded.

pp.   On margin: D. D. to JACOB MILLER 1784
221-   THIS INDENTURE made the 15th day of March 1779 Betwen WILLIAM BROOKS and
222   SUKY his Wife of the County of Culpeper of one part and JACOB MILLER of the
          County aforesaid Witnesseth that the said William Brooks and Sukey his Wife for
the sum 15 pounds 12 shillings current money of Virginia doth grant unto the said
Jacob Miller his heirs Fifty two acres of land in Culpeper County and St. Marks Parish
and bounded Begining at three pines in said Millers line Corner made for JOHN
SCHOOLER and runs thence North to one red oak saplin on a PATH side thence North
to 2 pines a Corner made for THOMAS GRAVES thence South to a pine on Mr. JAMES
TUTTs line thence with his line South to a white oak Corner to said Jacob Miller thence
with his line to the begining . . . .

                                                      William Brooks
   At a Court held for Culpeper County the 15th of March 1779
This Indenture ordered to be recorded.

pp.   On margin: D D Augst 14th 1783
223-   TO ALL PEOPLE We JOHN ZIMMERMAN JUNR. and KATHARINE his Wife of the
224   County of Culpeper send Greetings Know ye that for good causes but more for
          the love which we bear to our Eldest Son MICHAEL ZIMMERMAN and for his
better supoart in this world for the future we have given unto the said Mikel Zimmerman our Son his heirs Seventy acres of land in Culpeper County and Bromfield Parish
in the Great Fork of Rappahanock River and the same is bounded begining at 2 white
oaks and 1 red oak in JOHN HUFFANs line and runs thence with his line North to two red
oaks on a ridge thence West to a red oak and a pine in CHRISTOPHER ZIMMERMANs line
thence with his line West to two white oaks in Huffans line thence with his line South
to the begining place . . . . .

                                                      John X Zimmerman
   At a Court held for Culpeper County the 15th of March 1779   Katharine Zimmerman
This Indenture ordered to be recorded and the said Katharine
being first privily examined according to Law.

pp.   On margin: D D W. BRADLY 1790
224-   THIS INDENTURE made this 22nd day August 1777 Betwen GEORGE THORNTON and
228   MARY his Wife of the County of SPOTSYLVANIA of one part and ROBERT STRO-
          THER of the County of Culpeper Witnesseth that the said George Thornton and
Mary his Wife for the sum Two hundred pounds Virginia money doth grant unto the
said Robert Strother his heirs 4 Hundred acres in the County of Culpeper and Parish of
Bromfield in the Fork of the Hazel and Hughes Rivers and is bounded begining at a red

oak standing on the North bank of the Hughes River and Corner to ISAAC NORMAN just above the mouth of Spur Branch thence with Normans line North East to two white oaks near the MAIN ROAD another Corner to said Norman leaving Normans line runs up the several courses of the main road Vizt South to two red oaks on the Main Road thence South to two white oaks on the South side of the Main Road Corner to THOMAS HALL thence with his line South to two white oaks on the banks of the Hughes River thence down the several courses of the said River to the begining (Except two acres of land in the said Bounds belonging to the PARISH OF BROMFIELD whereon the BRUCK CHURCH now stands) . . . .

Presence of JOHN STROTHER,   George Thornton
     WILLIAM CHAMPE, JOHN THORNTON   Mary Thornton

The Commonwealth of Virginia to JOHN WALKER and JOHN SLAUGHTER Gent. Whereas George Thornton and Mary his Wife have sold unto Robert Strother Four hundred acres of land in the County of Culpeper and Whereas the said Mary cannot travil to our County Court to make ackowledgement of the said conveyance we give you power to examine her apart from her husband and when you have received her acknowledge-ment that you Certify us thereof in our said Court. Witness JOHN JAMESON Clerk of our said Court this 22nd day of August 1778 in the third year of the Commonwealth.

Culpeper Sct In Obedience to the within Commission we did go to the said Mary Thorn-ton and seperately from her husband did examine her and she did acknowledge the same this 22nd day of August 1778.

                         JOHN STROTHER   JOHN SLAUGHTER
At a Court held for Culpeper County the 19th of October 1778
This Indenture ordered to be Certified and at a Court held for the said County the 15th day of March 1779 was fully proved by two of the other witnesses and with the Com-mission thereto annexed and Certificate is ordered to be recorded.

pp.   THIS INDENTURE made the 15th of March 1779 Betwen HENRY LEWIS and
228-   RICHARD DICKEN of the County of Culpeper Executors of the Estate of CHRISTO-
231   PHER DICKEN deceased of the one part and BENJAMIN DICKEN of the County
        aforesaid Witnesseth that for the sum Sixty pounds current money of Virginia the said Henry Lewis and Richard Dicken they do hereby sell unto the said Benjamin Dicken his heirs forever two tracts of land in the said County and on the Water of the Robinson River and bounded Begining at a yew tree on the Robinson River thence down the several courses of the said river thence North to three chesnut oaks on a ridge that devides the said Benjamin Dicken and the said tract to the back line of the said tract on the FORK MOUNTAIN thence South to a parcel of Rocks on the top of the Fork Mountain thence North to the Begining containing One hundred and forty acres also one other tract of land containing Ninety acres begining at three white walnuts on the ROAD that leads to the DOUBLE TOP MOUNTAIN in a line of a tract that said Christopher Dicken Deceased left to his Son CHRISTOPHER DICKEN thence with the said line North to a Dogwood on the top of the ridge in the said line thence keeping the Ridge South East to a hikory to two chesnut oaks thence South to a Beech on a small Branch of the Robinson River call'd the Little River thence down the several courses of the said River to GEORGE WETHERALLs line thence with his line West to a red oak on the said road thence up the road to the begining . . . .

                                                        Henry Lewis
At a Court held for Culpeper County the 15th of March 1779   Richard Dicken
This Indenture with the Memorandum and Receipt ordered   John Dicken
to be recorded.

pp.   On margin: D D 1791 See Commission Recorded in Book R Folio 638

231-   THIS INDENTURE of Feoffment made the Fifteenth day of March 1779 Between

233   SAMUEL FARGESON and ANN his Wife of the County of Culpeper of one part and

WILLIAM NICHOLSON of the same County Witnesseth that Samuel Fargeson and
Ann his Wife for the sum of Twenty five pounds current money of Virginia have
granted unto said William Nicholson his heirs for ever a tract of land in the County of
Culpeper and in the North Little Fork of Rappahannock River being part of a larger
tract of land which said Samuel Fargeson purchased of JOHN WASHBORN and bounded
begining at three white oak saplins a Corner of HENRY SNITHERS in a line of JOHN
GREEN and runing thence with the said Snithers line North to a small chesnut oak a
Corner with Snither in a line of WILLIAM CORBIN thence South East to red oaks on the
North side of Cabin Branch in a line of EDMUND BROWNING thence with the said Brownings line South to a Pine Corner of John Green with Greens line North to the begining
containing Two hundred acres of land . . . .

Presents of JOHN WALKER.   Samuel Fargeon
           JOHN WIGGINTON   Ann Fargeson

  At a Court held for Culpeper County the 15th day of March 1779
This Indenture ordered to be recorded.

pp.   THIS INDENTURE made the 15th of March 1779 Betwen REGINAL BURDINE and

233-   ANN his Wife of the County of Culpeper of one part and WILLIAM CHAMPE of the

235   said County Witnesseth that said Reginal Burdine and Ann his Wife for the sum

Eighty pounds current money of the Commonwealth of Virginia have granted
unto said William Champe a parcel of land in County aforesaid bounded Begining at a
Double Chesnut in a line of one MERCHT. BOGLE runing thence South West to three
chesnut oaks on the South side of the Robinson MOUNTAIN and on the North side of the
North Branch of the Robinson River near the head thereof South East to a Chesnut Oak
on the South side of the said Mountain thence South to three chesnut oaks in the line of
the said Bogle thence with said Bogle South to the begining Including Two hundred and
ten acres of land . . . .

                                               Reginal Burdine
  At a Court held for Culpeper County the 15th day of March 1779   Ann Burdine
This Indenture ordered to be recorded.

pp   On margin: D D yr Ord: 1794

235-   THIS INDENTURE made this First day of March 1779 Betwen MORDECAI REDD and

240   AGATHA his Wife of the County of Culpeper of one part and GEORGE CALVERT of

     County aforesaid Witnesseth that said Mordecai Redd and Agatha his Wife for
the sum of Seven hundred and seventy five pounds current money of Virginia do sell
unto the said George Calvert Junr. land in County aforesaid and bounded begining at a
black oak in JOHN STROTHERs and CHAS. BROWNIGs line thence with Strothers line East
to a white wallnut on the Rush River thence up the River near the MILL thence North
up a Branch being the Dividing line between WILLIAM DAVIS and ROBERT STROTHER
thence with Davis line North to a black Stump West to a large Pine Corner to Davis and
the FULLER and GARWOOD thence with Garwoods line South to a Stump within the fence
thence North with SHEARWOODs line North to a large red oak on the ROAD side thence
South to some Maples in a branch near the Road Corner to CHS. BROWNING thence with
Brownings line South to the Begining containing Four hundred and thirty acres . . . .

Presence of us JOHN STROTHER,   Mordecai Redd
          JOHN SLAUGHTER, GEORGE JETT

The Commonwealth of Virginia to JOHN STROTHER, WILLIAM BROWN & JOHN SLAUGH-

TER Gent. Whereas Mordecai Redd and Agatha his Wife have sold land unto George Calvert junr. and Whereas the said Agatha cannot travel to our Court of Culpeper to make acknowledgement of the said conveyance we do give you power to personally go to the said Agatha and examine her apart from her husband and when you have received her acknowledgement that you Certify us thereof in our Court. Witness JOHN JAMESON Clk this First day of March 1779.

Culpeper SCT By Virtue of the within writ we caused the said Agatha Redd to come before us and examined her apart from her husband touching her acknowledgement of the Deed who freely acknowledged the same this 2nd day of March 1779.
                          JOHN STROTHER   JOHN SLAUGHTER
At a Court held for Culpeper County the 15th of March 1779
This Indenture was proved by two of the Witnesses thereto and ordered to be certified and at a Court held for the said County on the 17th of March 1779 was fully proved by a nother witness and with receipt endorsed Commission thereto annexed and Certificate is ordered to be recorded.

pp.   On margin: D D WM. JETT 1794
241-   TO ALL PEOPLE I WILLIAM JETT and SUSANNA my Wife send Greeting. Know ye
242   that I William Jett and Susanna my Wife of Saint Marks Parish in the County of
         Culpeper for natual love which we bear towards our loving Son EDGAR JETT of
Parish and County aforesaid have given unto our Son Edgar Jett and his heirs forever Two hundred acres of land conveyed to me by Deed from TOBIAS WILHOIT bearing date the 28th of November 1759 and is bounded Begining at a white oak standing in ROBERT BEVERLEY Esqr. Meander Run Mountain Tract on the GERMAN ROAD in a line of a Patent granted to MARTIN WALK and TOBIAS WILHOIT thence North to the Deviding line of THOMAS POINER decd to the begining ....
                                                         William Jett
At a Court held for Culpeper County the 19th of April 1779
This Indenture ordered to be recorded.

pp.   THIS INDENTURE made the 17th of April 1779 Betwen CHARLES BENSON and
242-   JUDITH his Wife of the County of STAFFORD of one part and HENRY BENSON of
246   the other part Witnesseth that the said Charles Benson and Judith his Wife for
         the sum Three hundred pounds current money of Virginia hath granted unto
the said Henry Benson and his heirs forever land in the County of Culpeper and bounded Begining at 2 white oaks on the South side of a branch of Heshmans Run and extending thence North East to the Begining containing Four hundred acres of land and granted to ALEXANDER HOWARD by Patent the 26th day of June 1731 and by the said Howard conveyed to the said Charles Benson ....
Presents of us: HARRIS HOOE,   Charles Benson
        EDWARD WEST, JOHN BENSON,   Judith Benson
        EDWARD WEST JUNR.
At a Court held for Culpeper County the 19th day of April 1779
This Indenture & the Memorandum thereon endorsed and with the Commission thereto annexed & Certificate is ordered to be recorded.
The Commonwealth of Virginia to CHARLES CARTER, GERARD BANKS and HARRIS HOOE Gent Whereas Charles Benson and Judith his Wife have sold unto Henry Benson land in the County of Culpeper and Whereas the said Judith cannot travil to our Court to make acknowledgement of the said Conveyance We give you power to go to the said Judith and examine her apart from her said husband and when you have received her acknowledgement that you Certify us thereof in our said Court. Witness JOHN JAMESON Clerk of

our Court the 17th day of April 1779 in the third year of the Commonwealth.
By Virtue of the within Commission we did personally go to the said Judith Benson and examined her apart from her husband who declared that she willingly consented and that she is willing the same should be recorded in the Court of Culpeper. Witness this 17th day of April 1779.

G. BANKS   HARRIS HOOE

pp. THIS INDENTURE made this tenth day of April 1779 Betwen JOSEPH EDDENS of the
246- Parish of St. Thomas and the County of ORANGE of one part and JOSEPH EDDENS
248 JUR. of County of Culpeper Witnesseth that the said Joseph Eddens for love he
beareth the said Joseph Eddens junr. as a Nephew hath granted unto said Joseph Edens junr. his heirs land in the County of Culpeper & Parish of Bromfield containing Two hundred and seventy acres the apple Orchard excepted during my life & bounded (to wit) by HENRY SHORTERs line one side and CAPT. ROBERTS line on the other side To have and to Hold the said Two hundred and seventy acres of land as a free and lawfull gift . . . .

In presents of us WILLIAM KIRTLEY,   Joseph Eddens
    ELIJAH KIRTLY, ADAM BANKS
    JONATHAN COWARD, WM. SIMS
At a Court held for Culpeper County the 19th day of April 1779
This Indenture with the Memorandum ordered to be recorded.

pp. THIS INDENTURE made this 15th day of May 1779 Betwen ROBERT FREEMAN JUNR.
248- of County of Culpeper and ANN his Wife of one part and JOHN FREEMAN Taylor
252 of the same County of other part Witnesseth that the said Robert Freeman for
the sum Eighty pounds current money of Virginia hath granted unto said John Freeman land in the Little Fork of the County of Culpeper being part of a tract of land formily granted to said Robert Freeman junr. by Deed from ROBERT FREEMAN SENR. his Father containing three hundred and eighty acres of land bounded Begining at a small white oak saplin on the West side of a branch Corner to HARRIS FREEMAN and runing with FRANCIS MORGANs line North to a red oak sapling on said Branch Corner to said Morgan and JESSE PASSON's line thence with Passon's line North to a hickory saplin Corner to WILLIAM BOWMER on the West side a hill thence with Bowners line South to a Stone Maple on the Mill Run thence down the Run the several courses below an old MILL thence up the said branch to a white oak Corner to Harris Freeman thence with his line North East to the begining . . . .

In presents of JAMES PENDLETON,   Robert Freeman junr.
    JOHN WIGGINTON, SAMUEL DILLARD   Ann Freeman
    WILLIAM HAYNIE
The Commonwealth of Virginia to JAMES PENDLETON, WM. McCLANAHAN and JOHN WIGGINTON Gent Whereas Robert Freeman junr. and Ann his Wife have sold to John Freeman land in County of Culpeper and Whereas the said Ann cannot travil to our County Court to make acknowledgement of the said conveyance we give you power to go to the said Ann and examine her apart from her husband whether she doth the same freely and when you have received her acknowledgement that you Certify us thereof in our said Court. Witness JOHN JAMESON Clerk this 15th day of May 1779 and year of the Commonwealth.
Culpeper Sct By Virtue of the within we did personally go to the said Ann Freeman and Examined her apart from her husband and she freely relinquished her right of dower and desired the same be recorded in the Court of Culpeper. Witness this 15th day

of May 1779.

JAMES PENDLETON   JOHN WIGGINTON

At a Court held for Culpeper County the 17th of May 1779
This Indenture with Memorandum and Receipt with the Commission thereto & Certificate thereon is ordered to be recorded.

pp.   On margin: D. D. to Ct. JAMESON 1787 p yr order

252-   THIS INDENTURE made this 21st day April 1779 Betwen RICHARD HACKLEY and

254   ELIZABETH his Wife of County of Culpeper of one part and ROBERT POLLARD of
       County aforesaid Witnesseth that said Richard Hackley and Elizabeth his Wife
for sum of two 271 pounds Current money of Virginia have sold unto the said Robert
Pollard his heirs forever Ninety two acres of land in County aforesaid on Potatoe Run
and bounded Begining at a hickory stump on said Run Corner to DANIEL BROWN thence
down the said run to the Mouth of a small branch know by name of Jack Pend Branch
Corner to Daniel Brown and Robert Pollard thence down Potatoe Run the several courses
to a Beach on the South side of the Run Corner to said Pollard and in Hackleys Lott line
thence leaving the said run and runing North to a pine in SPOTSWOODs back line
thence with his line South to the Begining . . . .
In presents of us CHARLES DAVENPORT,   Richd. Hackley
    EDWARD STEVENS, WILLIAM BRADLEY   Elisabeth Hackley

At a Court held for Culpeper County the 17th of May 1779
This Indenture and Receipt ordered to be recorded the said Elisabeth being first privily
examined according to Law.

pp.   THIS INDENTURE made this 17th of May 1779 Betwen ROBERT POLLARD of County

254-   of Culpeper of one part and WILLIAM PANNILL of County of ORANGE of other

256   part Witnesseth that said Robert Pollard for the rents hereafter mentioned have
      granted to Fairm Lett unto said Pannill during the turm of nine years from the
25 of December 1778 a certain piece of land in said County of Culpeper on Rapahanock
River suposed to contain about twenty acres bounded Begining at a cross fence which
devides the said Pannills part of the said from said Pollard in BROWNs line thence with
Browns lines to the river Rapahanock thence down the river to RICHARD HACKLEYs
Lott line thence with that Lott line to these cross fences betwen the said Pollard & Pannill thence with that Fence which runs nearly Parraral with the river about five hundred yeards to the begining containing about twenty acres or twenty five thousand
corn hills Common distance it being all the land that lyeth Betwen the said fence & said
river within the said lines said Pollard hath rented to said Pannill during the term of
nine years which said term will expire on the 25th day of December during the turm of
nine years from 25th Decem 1778 annual rent of five pounds current money of
Virginia . . . .

                                           Robert Pollard

At a Court held for Culpeper County the 19th of May 1779
This Indenture of Lease ordered to be recorded.

pp.   On margin: D D pr order 1812

256-   THIS INDENTURE made this 13th day of April 1779 Betwen JOSEPH EARLY of

258   Parish of Bromfield County of Culpeper of one part and ANGUS RUCKER of
      County aforesaid Witnesseth that said Joseph Early for the sum Fifty pounds cur-
rent money of Virginia hath granted unto said Angus Rucker his heirs Twenty acres of
land in the Parish and County aforesd bounded Begining at two chusnut trees on the
end of HOLTS MOUNTAIN thence North to two pines in EDDINS old line thence South with

a line of the said Ealys North to the begining . . . .
Presents of us JAMES EASTHAM,   Joseph Early
    RUSSELL VAWTER, JAMES OFFILL
  At a Court held for Culpeper County the 17th of May 1779
This Indenture ordered to be recorded.

pp.   THIS INDENTURE made this 4 day of February 1779 Betwen WILLIAM RUSSELL
258- of Parish of Bromfield and County of Culpeper of one part and JOSEPH EARLY
260   of Parish and County aforesaid Witnesseth that said William Russell for the sum
     350 pounds of good and lawfull money of Virginia hath granted unto Joseph
Early his heirs One hundred and twenty five acres of land in the Parish and County
aforesaid and bounded Begining at two white and one red oaks in a line of JOHN EDDINS
thence South West to the MAIN ROAD Corner to two white oaks at the head of the OLD
RACE PATH thence down the several courses of the FREDERICKSBURG ROAD East to Elk
Run Corner to two chusnuts bushes on bank of the said run on the East side of the run
to the begining . . . .
Presents of JAMES OFFILL,   William X Russell
    RUSSEL VAWTER, JOHN BREEDLOVE
  At a Court held for Culpeper County the 17th of May 1779
This Indenture ordered to be recorded.

pp.   On margin: D. D. P. EARLEY 1871
260- THIS INDENTURE mad the Seventeenth day of May 1779 Betwen JAMES OFFILL
263   and ANNAH his Wife of Parish of Bromfield and County of Culpeper of one part
     and JOSEPH EARLY of Parish and County aforesaid Witnesseth that the said James
Offill and Annah his Wife for the sum Two hundred pounds of good and Lawlfull money
of Virginia hath granted unto the said Joseph Early his heirs One hundred acres of land
being in the Parish & County aforesaid and bounded Begining at two red oaks in said
Earlys line thence with his lines to one red oak Corner with COLO. EPHRAIM RUCKER
thence South West with Offills old line to the begining . . . .
Presents of us JESSE VAWTER,   James Offill
    RUSSELL VAWTER, JOHN BREEDLOVE   Annah Offill
  At a Court held for Culpeper County the 17th of May 1779
This Indenture and Memorandum ordered to be recorded.

pp.   On margin: D D P. EARLEY 1871
263- THIS INDENTURE made this 17th of May 1779 Betwen EPHRAIM and ANGUS
265   RUCKER of Parish of Bromfield and County of Culpeper of one part and JOSEPH
     EARLEY of Parish and County aforesd of other part Witnesseth that said Ephraim
& Angus Rucker for sum of Two hundred pounds of good and Lawfull money of Virginia
hath granted unto Joseph Early his heirs Two hundred and Twenty acres of land being
in the Parish and County aforesaid and bounded Begining at one Locust thence South to
one red oak on the COURT HOUSE ROAD thence South to two red oaks on COLO. RUCKERS
ROAD thence along the said Road East to a branch in Earlys line with his lines to the
begining . . . .
Presents of us JAMES OFFILL,   Ephraim Rucker
    JAMES EASTHAM, RUSSELL VAWTER
  At a Court held for Culpeper County the 17th of May 1779
This Indenture and Memorandum ordered to be recorded.

pp.   On margin; D. D. P. EARLEY 1871
265-   THIS INDENTURE made the 16th of April 1779 Between ADAM GAAR of Parish of
268   Bromfield and County of Culpeper of one part & JOSEPH EARLY of Parish and
        County aforesaid Witnesseth that said Adam Gaar for sum of Eighty pounds cur-
rent money of Virginia hath granted unto the said Joseph Early his heirs One hundred
and twenty two acres and a half of land bounded Begining at a white oak in RUCKERs
line thence North to a white oak in a line of a Patent granted to MICHAEL HOLT thence
North to two pines in WILLIAM EDINS line thence South to the begining as also another
tract containing Thirty four acres bounded by part of the above line and COLO.
EPHRAIM RUCKERs line and the said Joseph Earlys line . . . .
Presents of us LEWIS GAAR,   Adam Gaar
      FRANCIS BLUNT, JAMES ✗ BURRELL
  The above are witnesses for Mr. Gaar.
      JAMES BARBOUR, WILLIAM EASTHAM,
      RUSSELL VAWTERS, JOHN BREEDLOVE
  At a Court held for Culpeper County the 17th of May 1779
This Indenture and Memorandum ordered to be recorded.

pp.   On margin: D D WM. TRIPLETT 1817
268-   THIS INDENTURE made this 17th of May 1779 Between WILLIAM DUNCAN and LUCY
271   his Wife, JOHN DAVISS and FRANCES his Wife of County of Culpeper of one part
        and PHILIP WEVER of aforesaid County of other part Witnesseth that William
Duncan and Lucy his Wife and John Daviss and Frances his Wife for sum of 200 pounds
current money of Virginia have sold unto sd Philip Wever his heirs Two hundred and
forty acres of land being in Culpeper County and Brumfield Parish granted to said
William Duncan and John Daviss by LORD FAIRFAX by Deed dated the 7th day of
December 1778 and Regester'd in the Proprietors Office in Book R folio 48 and bounded
as by a servey made by GEORGE HUME begining at three pines Corner to WILLIAM COON
thence with his line North to three red oaks by a Branch in WIDOW GREEN's line thence
with her line North to a forked white oak by the said Branch marked WG thence South
to two pines Corner to GEORGE WILLIAM FAIRFAX and to said Green & Coon thence with
Coons line North to an Imaginary Corner thence North to the begining containing two
hundred and forty acres of land . . . .
Presents of us JOHN STROTHER,   William Duncan Yr.
      JOSEPH EARLY, MORDICAI REDD   Lucy Duncan
                                         John Daviss
  Memorandum that on the 17th day of May 1779   Francis Daviss
Possession of the land was delivered unto within PHILIP WEAVER according to the
meaning of the within Deed . . .
      JOHN STROTHER   Wm. Duncan Yr.   John Daviss
      MORDICAI REDD   Lucy Duncan   Frankey Daviss
  At a Court held for Culpeper County the 17th of May 1779
This Indenture ordered to be recorded the sd Lucy and Frances being first privily
examined according to Law.

pp.   On margin: D. D. to GEO. HUME 1786
271-   THIS INDENTURE made the 15th of July 1778 Betwen BENJAMIN ZACHARY of
274   County of Culpeper and FRANKEY his Wife of one part and GEORGE HUME of the
        aforesaid County Witnesseth that for the sum of 100 pounds current money of
Virginia to Benjamin Zachary paid we do hereby acknowledge have sold unto the said
George Hume his heirs forever One hundred acres of land lying at the GREAT MOUN-

TAINS in Culpeper County and on the waters of the Robinson River and bounded Beg. on
a mountain side Corner to DOWNS in PHILIPS line now Corner to WILLIAM GRAYSON and
CHRISTOPHER CRIGLER thence North to a hickory on a mountain side thence East to a
Spanish oak on the North side of a branch South to a Dogwood Corner to NICHOLAS
CRIGLER and JOHN BREFOARD and in MARKs old line (so call'd) near a branch thence
West Corner cut down in an old field thence North to the begining . . . .
Presents of us GEORGE WILHOIT,   Benjamin Zachary
          ADAM X BARLER, JOHN HUME JUR.   Frankey Zachary
          GEORGE HUME
  At a Court held for Culpeper County the 17th of May 1779
This Indenture ordered to be recorded previous to which the said Frankey was first
privily examined according to Law.

pp.   THIS INDENTURE made the 17th of May 1779 Betwen JOHN WALLIS and BEHETHE-
274-   LAN his Wife of the County of Culpeper of one part and CHARLES HILL of the
276   same County Witnesseth tht said John Wallis and Behethelon his Wife for sum of
        Twenty pounds lawfull money of Virginia paid by the hands of ROBERT
EASTHAM and for other good causes said John Wallis and Behethelon his Wife have
granted unto Charles Hill his heirs forever land in County of Culpeper part of a tract of
Four hundred acres granted to JOSEPH COTTON by the right Honble THOMAS LORD FAIR-
FAX by Deed dated 27th day of May MDCCVL and bounded Begining at a white oak on the
North side of Thornton River opposite to the aforenamed Easthams MILL POND thence
down the said river to a white oak the said river thence North to three red oaks a
Corner of Thorntons thence West to two Spanish Oaks in a line of land whereon said
Wallis formily lived and now Mr. WM. COURTS and thence with said Courtses line South
to the Begining Including all that Plantation known by the name of JONES or CHEEKS
and containing one hundred acres . . . .
                                                                 John Wallis

  At a Court held for Culpeper County the 17th of May 1779
This Indenture ordered to be recorded.

pp.   On margin: D. D. to JNO. YAGER
277-   THIS INDENTURE made the 1 day of May 1779 Between JACOB BARLER of County of
279   ROCKINGHAM of one part and JOHN SMITH of County of Culpeper Witnesseth that
        said Jacob Barler for 100 pounds doth hereby sell unto said John Smith his heirs
for ever Ninety seven acres of land in the County of Culpeper on the branchs of White
Oak Run and bounded Begining at two white oaks extending thence North East to some
dead oaks on the side of a run thence West to the begining . . . .
Presents of us JAMES BARBOR,   Jacob Barler
        JOSEPH EARLY, JOSEPH WOOD JR.,
        ANDREW CARPENTER
  At a Court held for Culpeper County the 17th of May 1779
This Indenture ordered to be recorded.

pp.   On margin: D D to JNO. STRODE 1st Augt 1782
279-   THIS INDENTURE made this 23rd day of April 1779 Witnesseth that ZEDECKIAN
281   PROCTOR the Son of JOHN PROCTOR of the County of Culpeper and Parish of St.
        Marks hath of his own free and volenterely will or by and with the Consent of
his Father placed and bound himself apprintice unto ISRAEL ROBERTSON of County and
Parish aforesaid a Black Smith to be taught the trade sience or occupation of a black
smith which he the said Israel Robertson useth and with him as an aprintacne to dwell

and serve from the date of the date hereof unto the full end and term of two years and six months from the date hereof during all which time said apprintance his sd Master well and faithfully shall serve his secrets keep his lawfull Commands gladly obey hurt to his Master he shall not do nor wilfully suffer to be done by others, but the same shall forthwith give Notice to his said Master, the goods of his Master he shall not waste, nor them lend without his consent to any; at chards dice or any other unlawfull games shall not play, Taverns or Alehouses he shall not frequent fornication he shall not commit Matrimony he shall not contract from service of his said Master he shall not at ny time depart or absent himself without his said Masters leave,but in all things as a good faith-full Apprintance shall and will demean and behave himself towards his Master and all his, during said turm and said Master his said Apprintance the said trade sience or Occupation of a black Smith with all things thereunto belonging. shall and will teach and Instruct or cause to be well & sufficiently taught after the best way and manner that he can and shall also find unto his said apprintice meat drink washing Lodging & apparel both linnen and wollen and all other necessaries fit for such an apprintice during the term aforesaid and also the said Master shall alow the said Apprintice liberty of going to see his friends four times a year the said Apprintice is not absent himself from his said masters business in going home but only from Saterday Evening till Monday Evening and at the end of such turm shall give to his said Apprintice one hand hammer and one sledge hammer, also his said master is to forge the sd Apprintice a Vice but the said appurtaining is to find the Iron himself that takes to make the Vice and at expiration of time the said Master is to give the apprentice one new suite of apperal . . . .

Test DANIEL FARMER, JOHN STONE

                                                                    Israel Robertson
                                                                    Hezekier Proctor

   At a Court held for Culpeper County the 17th of May 1779
This Indenture of Apprentisteship was acknowledged & to be recorded.

pp.   THIS INDENTURE made the Fourth day of May 1779 Between WILLIAM BLEDSOE
281-   of Parish of Bromfield and County of Culpeper of one part and JOHN BLEDSOE
282   of Parish and County aforesaid Witnesseth that said William Bledsoe for 200
           pounds of good and lawfull money of Virginia to said William Bledsoe paid he
doth grant unto John Bledsoe his heirs one hundred acres of land in the Parish and County aforesaid and bounded begining at three pines corner in MEDLEYs line and runing thence South to two pines in BROOKINGs line thence along the said line North to two white oaks on the banks of GRIMEsis Run where CROSTHAIT ROAD crosses the said Run thence South to the Begining . . . .

                                                                    William Bledsoe

   At a Court held for Culpeper County the 17th day of May 1779
This Indenture Deed of Gift ordered to be recorded.

pp.   THIS INDENTURE made this 4 day of May 1779 Betwen WILLIAM BLEDSOE of
283-   Parish of Bromfield and County of Culpeper of one part and JOSEPH BLEDSOE of
284   Parish and County aforesaid Witnesseth that said William Bledsoe for sum of 190
           pounds of good and lawfull money of Virginia hath sold unto Joseph Bledsoe his
heirs One hundred acres of land in the Parish and County aforesaid and boundeth Be-gining at two white oaks corner to Land of TWYMANs and runing thence along his line North to two pines on a ridge thence South to two white oaks on the North side of a branch thence South to the begining . . . .

                                                                    William Bledsoe

At a Court held for Culpeper County the 17th day of May 1779
This Indenture Deed of Gift ordered to be recorded.

pp.   THIS INDENTURE made this 14th day of May 1779 Betwen JOHN ZACHARY of the
284-   County of Culpeper and ANN his Wife of one part and BENJAMIN ZACHARY of
287   aforesaid County Witnesseth that for the sum of 100 pounds current money of
         Virginia to the said Zachary Ser. have sold unto him the said Benjamin Zachary
his heirs forever Two hundred and forty acres of land lying in Culpeper County and on
the Waters of the Rapedan River and bounded Begining at a red oak standing on the
side of the MILL DAM Corner to JOHN ZACHARY JUNR. thence North to three pines on a
branch thence North to one pine near CAVES OLD ROAD thence up the said Road South
to two red oaks on the side of the Road on a top of the ridge, thence down the said Ridge
South to a Maple standing on the East side of Smith Run corner to MOSES BURBRIDGE
thence down the run to the begining . . . .
Presents of us JOHN WALKER,   John Zachary
 ARMISTEAD MINOR, WILLIAM BLEDSOE
   At a Court held for Culpeper County the 17th day of May 1779
This Indenture (with Memorandum and Receipt) ordered to be recorded.

pp.   On margin: D D to JOHN STROTHER Gent Aug 1780
287-   THIS INDENTURE made the 2nd day of December 1778 Betwen WILLIAM DAVIS
293   and SARAH his Wife of the County of Culpeper of one part and JOHN STROTHER
         JUNR. of County aforesaid Witnesseth that the said William Davis and Sarah his
Wife for the sum Two thousand pounds current money of Virginia they have granted
unto the said John Strother Junr. his heirs Eight hundred and fifty acres being the
tract of land purchased by the said William Davis of SARAH MINOR and JOHN MINOR
Executrix and Executor of the Last Will and Testament of JOHN MINOR Gent. of SPOTSYL-
VANIA COUNTY deceast and said land is in Culpeper County and Bromfield Parish in the
Little Fork of Rappahanock River joining on the Rush River on the East side thereof
and bounded Begining on the Rush River at a Corner of a tract of land lately belonging
to ROBERT STROTHER and runs with the line of that land to the line of a tract of land
lately the property of JOHN HASTEY thence with the lines of that land to a line of a tract
of land lately belonging to HENRY BACKER thence with the line of that land to the line
of a tract of land lately the property of JOHN PARKS JUNR. and now sold to the said John
Strother thence with lines of that land to the aforesaid Rush River thence up the
several courses of the said river to the begining place . . . .
Presents of JOHN STROTHER   William Davis
   JOHN SLAUGHTER, JOHN DAVIS   Sarah Davis
  The Commonwealth of Virginia to JOHN STROTHER, JOHN SLAUGHTER & GEORGE
WETHERALL Gent Greeting Whereas William Davis and Sarah his Wife by their certain
Indenture of Feeoffment have sold to John Strother Junr. land in Culpeper County and
Whereas the said Sarah cannot travel to our County Court of Culpeper to make acknow-
ledgement of the same we do give you power to go to the said Sarah and examine her
prively from her said husband whether she doth the same freely and when you have
received her acknowledgement that you Certify us thereon in our said Court. Witness
JOHN JAMESON Clerk of our said Court this 2d day of December 1778 in the third year of
the Commonwealth.
  Culpeper Sct By Virtue of the within Writ we causd the within mentioned Sarah Davis
to come before us & Examined her seperately from her husband touching her acknowledgement who freely acknowledged the same. In Witness this 2d day of December 1778.
                          JOHN STROTHER   JOHN SLAUGHTER

At a Court held for Culpeper County the 17th day of March 1779
This Indenture was partly proved and ordered to be Certified And at a Court held for the
said County the 17th day of May 1779 was fully proved & with a Commission and Certificate is ordered to be recorded.

pp.   On margin: D D to JNO. STROTHER Gent Augt. 1780
293-   THIS INDENTURE made the 2d of December 1778 Between JOHN PARKS and MARY
298   his Wife and MARY the Wife of RICHARD PARKS all of the County of Culpeper of
           one part and JOHN STROTHER JUNR. of the County aforesaid of the other part Wit-
nesseth that the said John Parks and Mary his Wife and Mary the wife of the said
Richard Parks for the sum Seven hundred and fifty pounds Current money of Virginia
paid by the said John Strother have sold unto the said John Strother Junr. his heirs
Four hundred and thirty eight acres of land in which Mary the Wife of Richard Parks
doth hold a right of dower and said land in Culpeper County and Bromfield Parish in the
Little Fork of Rappahanock River joining on the uper side of the LONG MOUNTAIN and
bounded Begining at two white oaks a Corner and uper Corner to land called COMPTON's
TRACT on the Rush River and runs thence with the line of that tract to a red oak
another corner to said Compton Tract thence North to a white oak on a Ridge thence
South East with a line of HENRY BACKERs and SANDSes to two pines on the side of the
ROUND MOUNTAIN in PEAYTONs line thence with his line South to a Double Chesnut on a
Ridge of the Long Mountain a Corner of Paytons thence leaving his line South to the
Rush River thence up the several courses of the said River to the begining place . . . .
In presence of JOHN STROTHER,   John Parks
        JOHN SLAUGHTER, WILLIAM C. BROWN   Mary Parks
    The Commonwealth of Virginia to JOHN STROTHER, JOHN SLAUGHTER and GEORGE
WETHERALL Gent Greeting Whereas John Parks and Mary his Wife and Mary Parks Wife
of Richard Parks have sold land in the County of Culpeper unto John Strother Junr. and
Whereas the said women cannot travel to our County Court of Culpeper to make ackowledgement of the same we do give you power to go to the said women and examine them
apart from their husbands whether they do the same freely and when you have received their acknowledgment that you Certify us thereof in our said Court. Witness
JOHN JAMESON Clerk of our said Court the 2d day of December 1778 and the third year of
the Commonwealth.
    Culpeper Sct By virtue of the within Writ we caus'd the within named Mary Parks to
come before us and examined her apart from her husband touching her acknowledgement of the Deed who freely acknowledged the same this 2nd day of December 1778.
                        JOHN STROTHER   JOHN SLAUGHTER
    At a Court continued and held for Culpeper County the 17th day of March 1779
This Indenture was proved by the Oaths of John Strother and John Slaughter two of the
witnesses thereto which is ordered to be Certified and at a Court held for the said County
the 17th day of May 1779 was together with the Memorandum and Receipt fully proved
by the Oath of WILLIAM COVINGTON BROWN and with the Commission annexed and
Certificate is ordered to be recorded.

pp.   On margin: D. D. to your Son RICHD. 1786
298-   THIS INDENTURE made this 17th day of May 1779 Betwen CHRISTOPHER ZIGLAR
302   and THOMAS YATES of the County of Culpeper of the one part and RICHARD
           CHILTON of aforesaid County of the other Witnesseth that for sum of Two hun-
dred pounds current money of Virginia to Christopher Ziglar and Thomas Yates paid we
do hereby acknowledge and have granted unto the said Richard Chilton his heirs forever Twenty one acres of land in the County of Culpeper Begining at a hickory on a

branch by ROAGUES ROAD in a line of CHRISTOPHER ZIMMERMANs thence North a long
the Road to three dead white oaks thence West to a white oak Corner to CHARLES BEN-
SONs thence South to a white oak in a line of the said Bensons thence to the Begining . .
In presents of JOHN GRAY,   Christopher Ziglar
                                                             Thomas Yates

   At a Court held for Culpeper County the 17th of May 1779
This Indenture (with Memorandum and Receipt) acknowledged by the parties and
ordered to be recorded.

pp.   On margin: D D to THO. BOHAM 1787
302-   THIS INDENTURE Witnesseth that WILLIAM GULLY and SALLY his Wife for and
303   in consideration of NEGROE Silva and fifty pound Cash Instantly one Cow and
         Calf one Ewe and Lamb one Sow with Pigg said Cow to be delivered at the time of
said William Gully Quiting Overseeing and going to house keeping hath sold and
Covenanted with said BOHANNAN and ANN his Wife both parties of the County of Culpeper and Parish of Bromfield all the Title of and to the Estate of GEORGE NUNN Deceased
as well the Estate of the said SALLY as her Brother BARNITT NUNNs Deceased right in
George Nunns Estate said Barnitt Nunn being dead, Salley being intermarried with
William Gully he the said Gully with Sally his Wife does hereby give up all rights to the
Estate of George Nunn to the said JOHN BOHANNON his heirs forever in consideration of
the things above mentioned To Hold all and Singular the Estate of George Nunn Decd
Except the land said Bohannon sold as the part assign'd his Wife during her natual life
by said George Nunn her former husband now wife to said Bohannan and the right by
agreement said Bohannon with his Wife transfer'd to TUNSTAL BANKS and one Negroe
supposed to be reasonable by just judgment above the age of six and under thirty years
of age at the Demise of the said John Bohannon all the Estate administred by ANN NUNN
Executrix and JOHN PENDLETON Executor of George Nunn Decd Estate and that hereafter
it shall be known and understood to all that their never shall be any further claim on
the Executors of the said George Nunn from me. In Witness this 12th day of November
1778.
In presents of us GEORGE WEATHERALL,   William TT Gully
       AM. BOHANNON, JOHN E GULLY,   Salley X Gully
       ELLIOT BOHANNON
   Recd. the within Consideration of Fifty pounds and one Negroe Girl Sylvia Received by
me this 12th day of Nobr. 1778.
                        Contract from Gully to Bohannon   William Gully
   At a Court held for Culpeper County the 16th day of Novr. 1778
This Indenture was proved by the Oath of GEORGE WEATHERALL a Witness thereto which
is ordered to be Certified and at a Court held for the said County the 13th day of
February 1779 was further proved by the Oath of ELLIOT BOHANNON which is also
ordered to be Certified and at a Court held for the said County the 17th day of May 1779
was further proved by the Oath of AMBROSE BOHANNON and ordered to be recorded.

pp.   THIS INDENTURE made the 26th day of October 1778 Betwen the honourable
304-   GEORGE WILLIAM FAIRFAX Esqr. by CRAVEN PEYTON his Attorney in fact of one
311   part and DAVID JAMESON JUNR. of Culpeper of the other part Witnesseth that
         said George William Faerfax for Rents and Covenants hereinafter mentioned on
part of the said David Jameson to be paid and performed hath granted to farm let unto
the said David Jameson his heirs Four hundred and sixty four acres of land in the
Parish of Saint Marks in the County of Culpeper on the Beaver Dam being part of a tract
of Two thousand two hundred and twenty five acres and bounded begining at a pine

Corner North on the point of a ridge extending thence with a line of the said Lot South to the line of the Paten the West side two small white oaks from one root thence with said line North to a pine near a small branch Corner to the patent thence with another of the said Corner thence another of the said lines North to the begining Containing Four hundred and sixty four acres with all profits excepting and preserving unto the said George William Fairfax all mines minerals and Quarries and the previledge of hunting and fowling upon any part thereof To Hold the said land unto the said David Jameson his heirs from the day of the date hereof during the natural lives of him the said David Jameson THOMAS JAMESON Son of JAMES JAMESON his Brother and JAMESON HAWKINS Son of JOHN HAWKINS paying yearly on the Tenth day of November 1778 the Rent of Thirteen pounds Eighteen shillings current money of Virginia and within the space of Six years at furtherest build or cause to be built on some convenient part a good dwelling house twenty feet by sixteen and a barn twenty feet square after the manner of Virginia building that they will also with six years plant an orchard of Two hundred winter apple trees at least thirty feet distance every way from each other and three hundred peach trees at sixteen feet distance every way from each other enclosed with a good fence keep them all well pruned and keep all said buildings, orchards and fences in good and sufficient repair and if at any time any timber fit for Carpenters or Coopers use or rails should be cut down in Clearing ground or other wise the same shall be worked up and not suffered to Rot or perish under the penalty of Five pounds current money over & above the value of such timber and that the said George William Fair Fax shall have free use of any part of the lands except the houses for the laying any of mines aforesaid to be got in the premises making full recompence to the said David Jameson for such loss and Moreover whenever Eight of the tenants shall by a Declaration in writing adjudge a PATH or ROAD needfull to be made through any part of the premises it may be lawfull for George William Fairfax to cause such path or road to be made . . . .

In presents of us SAMUEL CLAYTON JUNR.,   Go. William Fair Fax
      ROBERT POLLARD, JAMES SLAUGHTER JUNR.,
      JOHN CAMP, HENRY CAMP,
      GOODRICH LIGHTFOOT, ROBERT SLAUGHTER
  I do assign my right & title of the within land & premises to Mr. GEORGE NEWMAN given under my hand this twenty seventh day of October 1778.
Teste ROBERT LATHAM,   D. Jameson Jur.
      ANTHONY FOSTER, THOMAS LATHAM
  At a Court held for Culpeper County the 17th of May 1779
This Indenture of Lease ordered to be recorded.

pp.   On margin: DD to COLO. BARBOUR Sept 30th. 1780
311-   THIS INDENTURE made the 17th of June 1779 Betwen JOHN WAYLAND of one
312   part and GEORGE LAYMAN of other part Witnesseth that the said John Wayland
        for the sum of One hundred and seventy pounds hath granted unto the said
George Layman Two hundred and five acres of land in Culpeper County in the Robinson Fork of Rappahannock River and on Little Dark Run and bounded Begining at three white oaks a Corner of ADAM YEAGERs runing thence South to a Hickory Corner to BO-HANNON thence South to three Maples on a Branch thence South to two Box oaks to the Begining place . . . .

                                                               John Wayland

  At a Court held for Culpeper County the 21st of June 1779
This Indenture ordered to be recorded.

pp.   On margin; D..D. to J. JONES 1785
312-   THIS INDENTURE made the Seventh day of June 1779 Betwen RICHARD VERNON
314   of Culpeper County of one part and BENJAMIN QUINN of SPOTSYLVANIA COUNTY
        Witnesseth that said Richard Vernon for divers good causes but especially for
the natual love that he hath to the said Benjamin Quinn hath granted unto said Benjamin Quinn his heirs forever one tract of land in the County aforesaid it being part of
that tract whereon the said Richard Vernon Dwelleth and containing One hundred and
seventy three acres and bounded Begining at a Hickory saplin on Smith Run Corner to
Richard Vernon thence West to a hickory saplin on PENDLETONS PATH thence South to a
blased pine on a ridge Corner to the said Pendleton East to a white oak on a point Corner to BISHOP and THREALKEELs thence South to a red oak Corner to the said Bishop
thence to a pine Corner to Richard Vernon thence North to a white oak near a Branch
Corner to the said Vernon East to two red oaks on a rocky point near Smiths Run thence
up the said Run to the begining . . . .
Presents of BENJAMIN CAVE,   Richard Vernon
    RICHARD QUINN, JAMES QUINN
 At a Court held for Culpeper County the 21st day of June 1779
This Indenture ordered to be recorded.

pp.   On margin: D D J. STRODE May 96
315-   THIS INDENTURE made this 14th day of September 1778 Betwen GEORGE CARTER
318   and his Wife SALLEY CARTER of the County of STAFFORD of one part and HENRY
        FIELD and LEONARD BARNES of the County of Culpeper of other part Witnesseth
that for the sum of Five hundred pounds current money of Virginia to them paid said
George Carter & his Wife Salley Carter have sold unto them the said Henry Field and
Leonard Barnes their heirs forever two acres of land with the MILL and all improve-
ments upon it in aforesaid County and bounded Begining upon Mountain Run above the
PEAR HEAD at a Rock mark'd Æ runing thence North to a pair tree thence South East
to two Beaches on the bank of the run thence cross the Mill Tale up the said run North
to a thorn bush thence North to a thorn bush thence North to two white oaks on the
bank of the said Run to the begining . . . .
In presents of us JOHN JETT,   George Carter
    JOSEPH ROBERTS, DANIEL GREENWOOD
 The Commonweath of Virginia to THOMAS KEATH and JAMES BELL Gnt. Whereas George
Carter and Salley his Wife have sold Henry Field and Leonard Barnes two acres of land
and Mill with Appurtenances in Culpeper County and Whereas the said Salley cannot
travil to our County Court of Culpeper to make acknowledgement of the said conveyance we do give you power to personally go to the said Salley and examine her previly
apart from her husband whether she doth the same freely and when you have received
her acknowledgement that you Certifie us thereof in our said Court. Witness JOHN
JAMESON Clerk at the Courthouse this 21st of Decr. 1778 & third year of the Commonwealth.
 (See Certificate on other side)
 At a Court held for Culpeper County the 21st of Septr 1778
This Indenture ordered to be recorded. And at a Court held for the said County on the
21st day of June 1779 Examination of the said Sally Carter Commision for the privy was
returned into Court, and with the Certificate is ordered to be recorded.
 FAQR. SS: In Obedience to the within we have examined the said Salley Carter and find
that she acknowledgeth the deed annex'd bearing date the 14th day of September 1778.
Given under our hands and seal this 26th day of April 1779.
           THOMAS KEITH   JAMES BELL

pp.   On margin: D D J STRODE 1796
318-   THIS INDENTURE made this 14th day of September 1778 Betwen GEORGE CARTER
321   and his Wife SALLEY CARTER of the County of STAFFORD of one part and HENRY
           FIELD of County of Culpeper Witnesseth that for the sum one hundred and
Eighty pounds current money of Virginia to them the said George Carter and his Wife
Salley paid they hereby sold unto said Henry Field his heirs forever One hundred and
eighty four acres of land except two acres belonging to the MILL LOTT lying in the
aforesaid County and bounded begining at two white oaks on the bank of Mountain Run
by the mouth of a gulley thence South to Island of Thorney Branch thence North to two
hickory saplins by Thorney Branch standing among rocks thence West to two white
oaks by a small PATH thence South to two Box oaks in the line between GEORGE ROBERTS
and the land of Mr. JACESONs thence with the said line North to a white oak standing on
the bank of Mountain Run thence down the several courses to the Begining containing
Two hundred and eighty four acres of land except the two acres belonging to the Mill
Tract . . . .
Presents of us JOHN JETT,   George Carter
     JOSEPH ROBERTS, DANIEL GREENWOOD
  The Commonwealth of Virginia to THOMAS KEITH and JAMES BELL Gent Greeting
Whereas George Carter and Salley his Wife have sold unto Henry Field land in the
County of Culpeper and Whereas the said Salley cannot travel to our County Court to
make acknowledgement of the same we do give you power to receive the acknowledge-
ment she is willing to make and when you have examined her that you Certifie us
hereof in our Court. Witness JOHN JAMESON Clerk at the Courthouse the 21st day of
December 1778 and third year of the Commonwealth.
  FAUQR. SS: In Obedience to the within we have examined the said Salley Carter and
find that she acknowledged the   annext. Given this 26th day of April 1779.
                    THOS: KEITH   JAMES BELL
  At a Court held for Culpeper County the 21st day of Septr 1778
This Indenture was ordered to be recorded and at a Court held the 21st day of May 1779 a
Commission for the privy examination of the said Sally Carter was returned into Court
and with the Certificate is ordered to be recorded.

pp.   On margin. D D to PORTERS ordr Octr. 82
322-   THIS INDENTURE made this Eighth day of April 1779 Betwen FRANCIS THORNTON
325   and ANN his Wife of the County of SPOTSYLVANIA of the one part and SAMUEL
           PORTER of the County of FAUQUIER of the other part Witnesseth that said Fran-
cis Thornton and Ann his Wife for the sum six hundred pounds current money of Virginia have granted unto the said Samuel Porter his heirs land in the County of Culpeper
on the Little Fork of Rappahannock River which was granted by the Honourable
THOMAS LORD FAIR FAX unto the Reverend JOHN THOMPSON by Deed from the Proprie-
tary Office dated the 28th of October 1749 and bounded by lines & courses in the said
Deed and containing Eight hundred acres . . . .
Executed in presents of us WILLIAM THORNTON,   Francis Thornton
     THOMAS THORNTON, WILLIAM CHAMPE   Ann Thornton
  The Commonwealth of Virginia to FIELDING LEWIS, GEORGE THORNTON and CHARLES
DICK Gent. Greeting Whereas Francis Thornton and Ann Thornton his Wife have sold
unto Samuel Porter land in Culpeper County and Whereas the said Ann cannot travil to
our County Court to make acknowledgement of the same we do give you power to go to
the said Ann and examine her apart from her husband whether she doth the same
freely and when you have examined her that you Certifie us thereof in our Court. Wit-

ness JOHN JAMESON Clerk at the Courthouse this 16th day of November 1778.
    In Obedience to the within We the Subscribers did go to Mrs. Ann Thornton &
examined her privately & apart from her husband concerning the conveyance when
she informed us that she acknowledged the same freely and was willing the same be
recorded in the County Court of Culpeper. Given this 8th day of April 1779.
                              FIELDING LEWIS   GEO. THORNTON
    At a Court held for Culpeper County the 21st of June 1779
This Indenture with Commission & Certificate ordered to be recorded.

pp.   THIS INDENTURE made the 15th of June 1777 Betwen WILLIAM WARD and ANN
325-   his Wife of County of Culpeper and Parish of Bromfield of one part and WILLIAM
330   CHAMPE Gent of Parish and County aforesaid Witnesseth that said William Ward
        and Ann his Wife for sum Forty nine pounds Current money of Virginia have
granted unto said William Champe his heirs Three hundred and seventy acres of land in
Culpeper County and Bromfield Parish in the Great Fork of Rappahannock River under
the RAGGED MOUNTAIN is bounded Begining at two white oaks on the North fork of the
Beaverdam Run and by an old Corner formily the WIDOW JONESs runing thence with a
line of old marked trees North West to a Butterwood & red oak in Spigneal Hollow thence
South to three branched poplar in JOHN SAMPSONs line thence with his line North to a
white oak in a line formily the Widow Jones's thence with that line North to the
Begining the same being the tract of land whereon said William Ward now lives....
Presents of us WILLIAM GAINS,   William Ward
        THOMAS X LILLARD, BENJAMIN LILLARD   Ann X Ward
    The Commonwealth of Virginia to WILLIAM BROWN and JOHN SLAUGHTER Gent
Whereas William Ward & Ann his Wife have sold land in Culpeper County unto William
Champe and Whereas the said Ann cannot travel to our Court of Culpeper to make acknowledgement of the same we do give you power to go to the said Ann & examine her
apart from her husband whether she doth the same freely and when you have received
her acknowledgment that you certifie us thereof in our said Court. Witness JOHN
JAMESON Clerk at the Courthouse the 31st of July 1777 in the third year of the Commonwealth.
    By virture of the within Commission we did personally go to the said Ann and did
examine her seperate from her husband touching her acknowledgement and she declared that the did the same freely and was willing the same should be recorded in the
Court of Culpeper. Given this 12th day of June 1779.
                              WILLIAM BROWN   JOHN SLAUGHTER
    At a Court held for Culpeper County the 16th of June 1777
This Indenture with Memorandum and Receipt ordered to be recorded And at a Court
held for the said County the 21st of June 1779 this Commission thereto annexed & Certificate ordered to be recorded.

pp.   THIS INDENTURE made the 23rd day of April 1779 Betwen JOHN BERRY and
330-   JEMIMA his Wife of the County of Culpeper of one part and COLO. WILLIAM
334   CHAMPE of the County aforesaid Witnesseth that the said John Berry and
        Jemima his Wife for the sum Seventeen hundred and fifty pounds current
money of Virginia have sold unto the said William Champe his heirs One hundred and
seventy seven acres being the tract of land John Berry now lives on in Culpeper
County and Bromfield Parish joining on Pophams Run and LANDRUMs in the Great Fork
of Rappahannock River and bounded Begining at a white walnut stump on Pophams
Run Corner to said Champe and runs thence North to a hickory by a large PATH thence
North to a red oak Corner to MARSHALL thence South to a white walnut on the bank of

Landrams Run on the South side thereof thence South to Pophams Run thence up the
several courses of the said Run North to four Willows on the said Run Corner to
BENJAMIN LILLARD thence with his line North to the MAIN ROAD thence up the said
Road South to Pophams Run thence up the said run to the begining . . . .
In presents of us BENJAMIN LILLARD,   John Berry
    JAMES GRAVES, AMBROSE ADKINS   Jemima Berry
  At a Court held for Culpeper County the 21st of June 1779
This Indenture and the Memorandum & Receipt ordered to be recorded.

pp.   THIS INDENTURE made the Twenty third day of April 1779 Betwen JOHN BERRY
334-   SENR. and JEMIMA his Wife of the County of Culpeper of one part and BENJAMIN
336   LILLARD of the County aforesaid Witnesseth that said John Berry Senr. and
    Jemima his Wife for the sum Three hundred pounds current money of Virginia
have granted unto Benjamin Lillard his heirs for ever Twenty two acres of land and
three quarters in County aforesaid and bounded Begining at four Willows near the
bank of Pophams Run on the North side thereof Corner to Colo. WILLIAM CHAMPE and
runs thence North to the MAIN ROAD thence up the several courses of the Road South to
Pophams Run thence down the several courses of the said Run to the begining . . . .
In presents of us WILLIAM CHAMPE,   John Berry
    JAMES GRAVES, AMBROSE ADKINS   Jemima Berry
  At a Court held for Culpeper County the 21st day of June 1779
This Indenture & the Memorandum & Receipt ordered to be recorded.

pp.   On margin: D D J STRODE 1796
336-   THIS INDENTURE made this 9th day of June in the Fourth year of the Common-
340   wealth and 1779 Between LEONARD BARNS and his Wife SARAH BARNS & HENRY
    FIELD and his Wife JEANE FIELD of County of Culpeper and Parish of St. Marks
of one part & EDWARD VASS of aforesaid County and Parish of other part Witnesseth
that for the sum Three thousand pounds current money of Virginia the said Leneard
Barns and his Wife Sarah Barns and Henry Field and his Wife Jeane Field truely paid
have sold unto the said Edward Vass and his heirs forever Fifty acres of land in the
aforesaid County and Parish and on Mountain Run and bounded begining upon Mountain Run at JOSEPH SANFOARD Corner runing thence his line to Mr. LARKIN FIELD line
and from thence to the run and thence down the said Run to the begining. will at any
time at the reasonable request and proper charges of him the said Edward Vass make
any further conveyance that shall be by Law required to pass the Fee Simple Estate of
the land MILLS and premises from us to him . . . .
Test BENJAMIN ROBERTS Yonger   Leonard Barns
    BENJAMIN X PAYTON,   Henry Field
    DANIEL GREENWOOD   Sarah Barns
                                 Jenney Field
  The Commonwealth of Virginia to ROBERT GREEN, JAMES SLAUGHTER and RICHARD
WAUGH Gent Greeting Whereas Leonard Barns and Sarah his Wife and Henry Field and
Jenney his Wife have sold land in County of Culpeper to Edward Vass and Whereas the
said Sarah and Jenney cannot travil to our Court to make acknowledgement of the same
we give you power to go to the said Sarah and Jenney and examine them privily from
their husbands whether they do the same freely and when you have received their
acknowledgement that you Certifie us thereof in our said Court. Witness JOHN JAMESON
Clerk at the Courthouse the 20th day of October 1779.
  Persuant to the within Commission we have personally mett at the house of HENRY
FIELD JUNIOR and have privately examined his Wife Jenney Field who willingly ack-

nowledged her right of Dower and we have also examined the said Sarah Barns in like
manner who doth willingly acknowledge her right. Witness our hands this 13th of
November 1779.   ROBERT GREEN   RICHARD WAUGH
  At a Court held for Culpeper County the 21st of June 1779
This Indenture ordered to be recorded And at a Court held for the said County the 15th
day of November 1779 the Commission thereto annexed and the Certificate was returned & ordered to be recorded.

pp.   THIS INDENTURE made the Twenty first day of June 1779 Betwen JAMES WILSON
340-   and LYDIA his Wife of the County of Culpeper of one part & AMBROSE POWELL of
342   the aforesaid County Witnesseth that said James Wilson and Lydia his Wife for
        the just sum of Forty pounds current money of Virginia hath granted unto the
said Ambrose Powell in his actual possession by Indenture of Lease by virtue of the
Statute for Transferring uses into possession land in Culpeper County and bounded begining at two pines Corner to Ambrose Powell in James Wilsons line thence South to
three pine standing on the North side of the Ess Branch thence down the said Branch
North in a line of CHARLES HUME thence with his Line North to a pine Corner to said
Powell and Hume thence with a line of said Powells to the Begining . . . .
                                                        James Wilson
  At a Court held for Culpeper County the 21st day of June 1779
This Indenture and Receipt ordered to be recorded.

pp.   On margin: Dld. to THO. S. LONG 1804 April
342-   THIS INDENTURE made the 6th day of October 1774 Betwen FIELDING LEWIS,
345   WILLIAM ROBINSON, WILLIAM FITZHUGH of Someset, WILLIAM FITZHUGH of
        Marmion, JOSEPH JONES, JOHN SKENKER, LEWIS WILLIS & CHARLES WASHINGTON
Esqr. of one part and MARK THOMAS of County of Culpeper of other part Witnesseth that
Whereas by an Act of the General Assembly passed in the Seventh year of the Reign of
his Present Majesty King George the third Certain lands held by CHARLES CARTER Esqr.
of KING GEORGE COUNTY whereof he stands seized in tale Maile which lands were by the
said Act vested in said (those named) and the sevever of Servevors of them in Trust to
be sold by them for the purposes in the said Act and Whereas the Trustees have con-
tracted with the said Mark Thomas for One hundred and fifty acres of the lands mentioned and being part of the tract of land commonly called by the name MOUNT PONE for
the Consideration of Sixty five pounds current money of Virginia NOW THIS INDENTURE
WITNESSETH that persuant to the power given the said Trustees and for the sum of Sixty
five pounds current money of Virginia to them paid by the said Mark Thomas they the
said (Trustees named) have sold unto Mark Thomas One hundred and fifty acres
includeing the Plantation whereon the said Mark Thomas now lives bounded begining
at a Gum corner to the Old Patent thence South East to two small Maples on a branch
Corner to ZIMMERMAN the same course continued to a stump thence South to the
Begining . . . .
In Presents of us   Fielding Lewis
  B. JOHNSTON as to FL, WR, WF-S, JS, LW & WF-M   Wm. Robinson
  BIRKETT DAVENPORT as to the above & JS   Wm. Fitzhugh
  WILLIAM THORNTON Do   Wm. Fitzhugh
  WILLIAM KIRTLEY to the above except JS   Jos. Jones
  WILLIAM KIRTLEY & as to WF-M   J. Skinker
  PHILIP CLAYTON JUNR. - JS   Lewis Willis
  FRENCH STROTHER - JS   Chs. Washington
  JOHN ROSE

At a Court held for Culpeper County the 13th of May 1775
This Indenture was partly proved which is ordered to be Certified and at a Court held
for the said County the 21st day of June 1779 was fully proved and ordered to be
recorded.

pp.   THIS INDENTURE made this 19th day of June 1779 Between JOSHUA WILLIS and
345-   SARAH his Wife of the County of Culpeper of one part and THOMAS PORTER of
347   the aforesaid County Witnesseth that for the sum Three hundred pounds current
             money of Virginia they have sold unto the said Thomas Porter his heirs forever
Two hundred acres of land in the aforesaid County and bounded begining at two white
and one red oak Corner to the sd Porter in the old ISLAND line and runing thence South
to a red oak on the top of a Mountain thence North to the begining . . . .
Presents of us JOSEPH WOOD JUNR.,   Joshua Willis
     BENJAMIN FINNELL, ROBERT ALCOCK
  At a Court held for Culpeper County the 21st of June 1779
This Indenture ordered to be recorded.

pp.   THIS INDENTURE made the Twentieth day of February 1779 Between PHILIP
348-   HARPINE and CATR. his Wife of the County of SHERRIDORE in Colony of Virginia
351   of the one part and JOHN LILLARD of the County of Culpeper of the other part
             Witnesseth that said Philip Harpine and Catr. his Wife for the sum seven hun-
dred and seventy five pounds current money of Virginia have sold unto the said John
Lillard his heirs forever Nine hundred and ninety three acres of land in the County of
Culpeper and is bounded Begining at a blazed white oak on a Ridge on the North side of
THORNTONS ROAD in a line of JOHN HUGHS now COLO. THORNTON runing thence North to
a red oak on the South side of the Hazel River at the foot of a great rock thence up the
several courses of these rivers to two learge white oaks one of which is marked **E**
on the North side of Cabbin Branch thence up the several Courses of said Branch to two
Spanish oaks Corner to Thornton thence leaving Thornton thence with that line North
to Thorntons Road thence with line of Hughs to the Begining . . . .
In presents of BENJAMIN LILLARD,   Philip Harpine
     CHARLES CLIFTON, JOHN BRADLEY,   Catr. Harpine
     JOSEPH MOORE
  The Commonwealth of Virginia to TAVERNER BEALE and MARTIN NALL Gent Whereas
Philip Harpine and Catr his Wife have sold to John Lillard land in the County of Culpeper and Whereas the said Catr cannot travel to our County Court to make acknowl-
ledgement of the same we do give you power to personally go to the said Catr and examine her apart from her said husband whether she doth the same freely and when you
have received her acknowledgement that you Certify us thereof in our said Court. Witness JOHN JAMESON Clerk of our Court the day of 1779 and year of the Commonwealth
  Persuant to the within Commission we Taverner Beale and Martin Nall Gent personally
went to CATHARINE HARPINE Wife of PHILIP HARPINE and examined her apart from the
said Philip Harpine touching her consent to the Indenture which she gives her free
consent to the same & further is willing should be recorded in the County Court of Culpeper. Given this 16th day of June 1779
                         TAVERNER BEALE   MARTIN NALL
  At a Court held for Culpeper County the 21st of June 1779
This Indenture and Memorandum and Receipt with the Commission and Certificate
ordered to be recorded.

pp.   On margin: D. D. to DANL. ALBETT Dec 7th 1784
352-   THIS INDENTURE made the 21st of June 1779 Betwen JAMES LILLARD of the
354   County of Culpeper & KEZIAH his Wife of one part and JOHN BROWN of the said
         County Witnesseth that for the sum Fifty five pounds current money of Virginia
to him paid by the said John Brown doth hereby acknowledge and do grant unto the
said John Brown land on the Hughs River in the said County containing One hundred
and Fifteen acres and bounded Begining at two Chesnut oaks on the side of a Mountain
JOHN GRAVES Corner & runing thence with his line North to the Hughs River and
twelve poles farther to a small hickory in the said Graves line thence leaving his line
North to a chesnut on a point of a Mountain thence South to a chesnut oak on a Stoney
point and twenty two poles farther near the top of the Mountain on the falling grounds
of the Hughs River & thence South to the begining . . . .

                                                          James Lillard
  At a Court held for Culpeper County the 21st of June 1779   Keziah Lillard
This Indenture ordered to be recorded the said Keziah being
first privily examined as the Law directs.

pp.   THIS INDENTURE made the 20th of June in the Year One thousand seven hun-
354-   dred & Seventy ( ) Betwen BRYANT MEGRATH and MARY his Wife of the County
357   of Culpeper of one part and JOHN MACKENNEY of the County and Parish afore-
         said Witnesseth that the said Bryant Megrath and Mary his Wife for the sum
Forty pounds current money of Virginia have granted unto the said John Mackenney
his heirs Fifty acres of land in Culpeper County and Bromfield Parish in the Goardvine
Fork of Rappahannock River and joining on the main RED OAK MOUNTAIN the same
being part of Two hundred and thirty eight acres of land granted to Bryant Megrath by
the right honarable THOMAS LORD FAIR FAX Proprietor of the Northan Neck in Virginia by Deed from the Proprietors Office bearing date the third day of August 1778 and
said Fifty acres is bounded begining at two Chusnuts oaks on a rock in the line of
CHARLES MOZINGO and runs with his line North to a Double Chesnut near the top of a
small Mountain thence Leaving that line North to two small hickories at the foot of the
said Mountain in or near SERGANTs line thence with that line South in said line Corner to JOHN MACKENNEY deceast then with his line South to the begining . . . .
Presents of us REGINAL BURDINE,   Bryant Magrath
         CHARLES DAVENPORT
  At a Court held for Culpeper County the 21st day of June 1779
This Indenture with the Memorandum & Receipt endorsed ordered to be recorded.

pp.   On margin: Ded to A M SMITH for R. YOWELL
357-   THIS INDENTURE made the 21st day of June 1779 Betwen JOSEPH JAMES JUNR. and
360   ELIZABETH his Wife of County of Culpeper of one part and WILLIAM CHAMPE
         Gent of the County aforesaid Witnesseth that said Joseph James and Elizabeth his
Wife for the sum Twenty pounds current money of Virginia have sold unto the said William Champe his heirs Nine acres of land in Culpeper County and Bromfield Parish in
the Great Fork of Rappahannock River joining on Hughes River bounded begining at a
hickory on the bank of Hughes River on the South side thereof a Corner to said Joseph
James and William Champe and runs thence up the several courses of the said river as
North to two red oaks on the said river near the lower end of an Island South to a red
oak in a line betwen said James and Champe thence with that line to the Begining place
 . . . .

                                                          Joseph James jr.

At a Court held for Culpeper County the 21st of June 1779
This Indenture (with Memorandum and Receipt) ordered to be recorded.

pp.   On margin: Ded. to A. M. SMITH for R. YOWELL
360-   THIS INDENTURE made the 21st of June 1779 Betwen JOSEPH JAMES JUNR. and
363   ELIZABETH his Wife of County of Culpeper of one part Witnesseth that said
          Joseph James and Elizabeth his Wife for sum Sixty pounds current money of Vir-
ginia to them paid by the said WILLIAM CHAMPE have granted unto the said William
Champe his heirs Forty five acres of land in Culpeper County and Bromfield Parish in
the Great Fork of Rappahannock River joining on the North side of Landrums Run and
bounded Begining at two Gums on the said Run a Corner to said Champe and James runs
thence with their line North West to a fork of a small branch thence down the said
branch South to said Landrums Run thence down the several courses of the said Run to
the Begining . . . .

                                                                        Joseph James jur.

At a Court held for Culpeper County the 21st of June 1779
This Indenture (with Memorandum and Receipt) ordered to be recorded.

pp.   THIS INDENTURE made the 21st day of June 1779 Betwen WILLIAM CHAMPE Gent
264-   and MARY his Wife of County of Culpeper of one part and JOSEPH JAMES JUNR. of
367   County aforesaid Witnesseth that said William Champe and Mary his Wife for
          sum of Sixty pounds current money of Virginia have sold unto said Joseph James
his heirs Seventy six acres and three quarters of land in Culpeper County and Bromfield Parish in the Great Fork of Rappahannock River and betwen the Hughes River
and Landrum Run and same is bounded begining at two red oaks in a line betwen the
said James and Champe and thence South to two red oaks near an old field thence North
to a white oak in the aforesaid line betwen said James and Champe thence with that line
to the begining place . . . .

                                                                        William Champe

At a Court held for Culpeper County the 21st of June 1779
This Indenture (with Memorandum and Receipt) ordered to be recorded.

pp.   On margin; D. D. JNO. FISHBACK Exor of CLORE 1819
367-   THIS INDENTURE made the 21st of June 1779 Between MICHAEL SWINDLE and
369   ELIZABETH his Wife of Bromfield Parish and County of Culpeper of one part and
          MICHAEL CLORE of the Parish and County aforesaid Witnesseth that said Michal
Swendal and Elizabeth his Wife for sum One hundred pounds current money of Virginia
hath granted unto said Michael Clore his heirs Eighty five acres of land in Parish and
County aforesaid Begining at three white oaks standing on Slaughters Run thence
North to one Poplar on the said Run and in the said Swendals line thence with his line
South to two pines Corner to JOHN SEALEs and TIMOTHY SWINDAL thence with Swindals
line North East to a Stone at HENDERSONS PEN thence with his line North up the said
Run to the begining . . . .

                                                            Michael Swindle
At a Court held for Culpeper County the 21st of June 1779   Elizabeth ✗ Swindle
This Indenture ordered to be recorded previous to which the
said Elizabeth was first privily examined according to Law.

pp.   THIS INDENTURE made this 21st of June 1779 Betwen MICHAEL CLORE and MAR-
369-   GRET his Wife of County of Culpeper of one part and MICHAEL SWINDAL of afore-
371   said County Witnesseth that said Michael Clore and his Wife hath agreed toge-

ther to Exchange a certain peace of land containing One hundred and fifty acres whereof we do Exchange unto him the said Michal Swindal his heirs a certin peace of land in Culpeper County Begining at a Corner a Great Rock Corner to GEO. LONGs Corner then the several courses up the river to the mouth of White Oak Run to CARPENTERs line, thence up the said line South to the begining . . . .

                                                                    Michael Clore
                                                                  · Margret ✗ Clore

At a Court held for Culpeper County the 21st of June 1779
This Indenture ordered to be recorded previous to which the
said Margret was first privily examined according to Law.

pp.   On margin: D D to Mr. BISHOP Jany. 1785
371-   KNOW ALL MEN by these presents that I ABRAHAM HAINES of Evesham Town-
373   ship in the County of BUCKLINGTON in the State of WEST NEW JERSEY Yeoman for
        divers good causes have apointed by trusty friend JONATHAN BISHOP of Culpeper
County in the State of Virginia Yeoman my true and lawfull Attorney to lease let set or
demise all of my lands in Culpeper County aforesaid to any person for such term of
years as he shall think fit and for that purpose to make any lease or leases which shall
be required for leasing granting my said Attorney my full power to take all means after
the leasing of said premises for receiving all said rents when shall become due and if
need be to enter into any part of said premises and there make Distress sufficient to
satisfie all the said rents when shall be in arrear & upon recoveries of the rents or
sums of money to make acquittances for the same and also perform all other things
needfull in and about the premises as I my self might do. In Witness whereof I have set
my hand and seal the Ninth day of November 1778.
In presents of CALEB CRISPIN,   Abraham Haines
        ABRAHAM SHOEMAKER
 Memorandum May the 27th 1779 This Day the above Abraham Haines acknowledged
the above to be his hand & seal & this Power of Attorney to be his Act and Deed in
presence of us   DAVID JAMESON JUNR., GOODRICH LIGHTFOOT
 At a Court held for Culpeper County the 21st of June 1779
This Power of Attorney ordered to be recorded.

pp.   On margin: D D to Self April 1785
373-   THIS INDENTURE made this 11th of June 1779 Betwen ALEXANDER McQUEEN JUNR.
375   of County of Culpeper of one part and JAMES WHITEHEAD of the same County
        Witnesseth that said Alexander McQueen for sum Fifty two pounds Ten shillings
hath granted unto the said James Whitehead his heirs land in said County adjoining the
Plantation whereon the said James Whitehead now lives Begining at one box oak Corner
to said Whitehead and Mr. BERKETT DAVENPORT runing thence North to two white oaks
in said Davenports line thence North to the begining containing Seventeen acres and
one half of land . . . .
Presents of us JAMES PENDLETON,   Alexander McQueen
        SAMUEL CLAYTON, WILLIAM McQUEEN
 At a Court held for Culpeper County the 21st day of June 1779
This Indenture ordered to be recorded.

pp.   THIS INDENTURE made the 19 day of July 1779 Betwen BENJAMIN LOWEN of
375-   County of Culpeper of one part and FRANCIS LOWEN of County aforesaid Witnes-
377   seth that said Benjamin Lowin for natual love and Effection he has unto said
        Francis Lowin his Brother as for the sum of Five Shillings current money have
given unto said Francis Lowins and to his heirs land in the County of Culpeper con-

taining Two hundred and Eighteen acres and is bounded Begining at two small beaches and an oak on Cedar Run Corner to DANIEL GENNEN thence with his line North to two small white oaks Corner to said Ginnan thence with his line North to a white oak Corner to GOODRICH LIGHTFOOTs line thence with his line to a white oak Corner to SPOTSWOODs and Lightfoots thence the same course to two white oaks in JOHN SPOTSWOOD line thence with his line South RICHARD REYNOLDS line thence with his line East to an old field Corner to Reynolds and ALLAN thence South to a white oak Corner to Richard Reynolds on Cedar Run thence down the said Run to the begining. In Witness whereof said Benjamin Lowen hath set his hand and seal.

Ben. Lowen

At a Court held for Culpeper County the 19th of July 1779
This Indenture ordered to be recorded.

pp.   THIS INDENTURE made this 15th of July 1779 Betwen CHRISTOPHER TANNER and
377-   ELIZABETH his Wife of County of Culpeper of one part and HENRY AYLOR of
379   County aforesaid Witnesseth that for sum Twenty pounds current money of Vir-
         ginia to said Christopher Tanner and Elizabeth his Wife they do hereby ack-
nowledge have sold to the said Henry Aylor his heirs for ever Thirty four acres of land in County aforesaid and bounded Begining at a Spanish oak in the Robinson River thence up the said river North to a white oak on the South side of the Robinson River at the mouth of Mullatts Run thence up the said run South to the begining . . ..
In presents of JOHN HUME,   Christopher Tanner
     MARK FINKS, STEPHEN FISHER
     At a Court held for Culpeper County the 19th of July 1779
This Indenture (with Memorandum and Receipt) ordered to be recorded.

pp.   On margin: D. D.. 88
379-   THIS INDENTURE made this 17th of July 1779 Betwen HENRY ALER and MARGA-
382   RET his Wife of County of Culpeper of one part and THOMAS PORTER of aforesaid
         County of the other part Witnesseth that for the sum Seven hundred pounds
current money of Virginia to them the said Henry Aler and Margaret his Wife in hand paid they do hereby acknowledge have sold in feeoff the said Thomas Porter his heirs forever land containing One hundred and sixty two acres in the said County on both sides of the Robinson River and bounded begining at a white oak thence North to three pines Corner to JACOB HUFMAN and FREDERICK TANNER thence with said Tanner line South to the river thence up the several courses of the said Robinson River to a white oak on the South side said river near the mouth Alers Old Mill Run thence South to a forked Chesnut on the said Mill Run thence South the Corner down near the said Alers old Dam on the said run thence South to a white oak in Clear'd ground Corner to ROUZY thence North to GEORGE COOKs line thence with said Cook South to JOSEPH WILLIS's line thence with said Willis's line North East to said Willis's thence to the begining also one other parcel of land in the aforesaid County containing One hundred and sixty three acres of land and bounded begining at a red oak Corner to said JOSHUA WILLIS thence with said Willises line North to a pine on the side of a hill thence South to a chesnut oak on the West side of a Mountain thence North to the begining . . . .
Presents of us JOHN HUME,   Henry Aylor
     STEVEN FISHER, MARK FINKS   Margaret + Aylor
     At a Court held for Culpeper County the 19th of July 1779
This Indenture with memorandum and receipt ordered to be recorded.
     At a Court held for the said County the 21st of May 1781 MARGARET AYLOR came into

Court & acknowledged the within conveyance being first previly Examd. according to Law.

pp.   On margin: D D Self 1801
382-   THIS INDENTURE made this 19th day of July 1779 Betwen JOHN BACK and MAR-
384   GRET his Wife of County of Culpeper of one part and PETER CLORE of aforesaid
         County Witnesseth that for sum Twenty pounds current money of Virginia the
said John Back and Margret his wife do hereby acknowledge have sold unto the said
Peter Clore his heirs forever Twenty acres of land in the aforesaid County and bounded
Begining at four Pessimmons trees on Deep Run thence down the run North to two
chesnut one the North side the Robinson River thence down the several courses of the
said River to a Gum at the Mouth of Deep Run thence up the said run to the begining ...

                                                           John X Back
At a Court held for Culpeper County the 19th of July 1779   Margret X Back
This Indenture (with Receipt and Memorandum) orderd to be
recorded previous to which the said Margret was first privily examined according to
Law.

pp.   THE COMMONWEALTH OF VIRGINIA to ROWLAND THOMAS and CATLETT CONWAY
384-   Greeting Whereas WILLIAM HUNTER and SARAH his Wife by their Indenture
385   the 5th day of July 1775 have sold unto WILLIAM RICE One hundred and eighty
         eight acres of land in County of Culpeper and Wheras the said Sarah cannot
travel to our County Court of Culpeper to make acknowledgement of the same we do
Command you that you go to the said Sarah and receive her acknowledgement apart
from her husband whether she doth the same freely and when you have examined her
as aforesaid that you Certify us thereof in our said Court. Witness JOHN JAMESON Clerk
of our said Court at the Courthouse the first day of May 1778 in the second year of the
Commonwealth.
By Virtue of the Commission we the Subscribers did on the 9th day of July 1779 go to
SARAH HUNTER and having examined her privately and apart from her husband do
Certify that she declared it was without his threats and freely acknowledged the Con-
veyance & was willing the same be recorded in the County Court of Culpeper.
                         ROWLAND THOMAS   CATLETT CONWAY

pp.   THE COMMONWEALTH OF VIRGINIA to ROWLAND THOMAS and CATLETT CONWAY
386-   Greeting Whereas WILLIAM HUNTER and SARAH his Wife by their Indenture the
387   5th day of July 1775 have sold unto EDWARD TINSLEY One hundred and eighty
         five acres of land in County of Culpeper and Whereas the said Sarah cannot
travel to our County Court of Culpeper to make acknowledgement of the same we do
command you that you go to the said Sarah and receive her acknowledgement apart
from her husband whether she doth the same freely and when you have examined her
as aforesaid that you Certify us thereof in our said Court. Winess JOHN JAMESON Clerk of
our said Court and the Court house the first day of ( ) 1778 in the second year of the
Commonwealth.
ORANGE to wit: By Vertue of the Commission within mentioned we the Subscribers did
on the Ninth day of July 1779 go to Sarah Hunter and having examined her privately
from her husband do certifie that she declared it was without the persuasion or threats
of her said husband she freely acknowledged the Conveyance and was willing the same
should be recorded in County Court of Culpeper.
                         ROWLAND THOMAS   CATLETT CONWAY

pp.   On margin: D D to JNO WILLIAMS 24th Mar 1783
387-   THIS INDENTURE made the 16th of August 1779 Betwen JOHN GRIGSBY of County
389   of Culpeper and ELIZABETH his Wife of one part and ALEXANDER DOWNEY of
         County of ORANGE Witnesseth that said John Grigsby and Elizabeth his wife for
sum of Three thousand six hundred pounds Current money of Virginia have granted
unto the said Alexander Downey his heirs land in the County of Culpeper containing
Three hundred and eighty five acres of land bounded Begining at two oaks Corner to
ALFRED HEAD thence with his line South to two hickories saplins on the Rapaddan
River Corner to said Head thence down the said river to a white oak Corner to WILLIAM
ROBESON thence with his line North to a pine on the side of the Mountain thence with
said line North to three small pines near a PATH thence North to a chesnutt oak on the
side of the Mountain called the ROUND MOUNTAIN thence South to a Gum in Heads line
thence with them lines North to the begining . . . .

                                                              John Grigsby
    At a Court held for Culpeper County the 16th day of August   Elizabeth Grigsby
1779 This Indenture ordered to be recorded previous to which
the said Elizabeth was privily examined as the Law directs.

pp.   On margin: D D A. COLEMAN 1789
390-   THIS INDENTURE made the 16th of November 1778 Betwen JOSEPH JAMES Gent of
392   County of Culpeper and MARY his Wife of one part and AMBROSE COLEMAN of
         the other part Witnesseth that said Joseph James and Mary his Wife for the sum
Sixty four pounds current money have granted unto said Ambrose Coleman his heirs
forever land hereafter mentioned One hundred acres in the County of Culpeper and a
part laid of by said James being part of said tract of land said James now lives upon
called the FOX MOUNTAIN TRACT Begining at three white oaks thence South to two pines
in FIELDs line thence South to a box oak in WRIGHTs line from thence along Wrights
line to the begining . . . . .
Presents of us EDMD. TERRILL,   Joseph James
         THOMAS BROWN, ROBERT COLEMAN
    At a Court held for Culpeper County the 16th day of August 1779
This Indenture (with Receipt) ordered to be recorded.

pp.   THIS INDENTURE made this 16th day of August 1779 Betwen EPHRAEM KLUGH and
392-   CONRAD DELPH of one part and ZACHARIAH SIMS of other part Witnesseth that
394   they the said Ephraim Klugh and Conrad Delph & MARY his Wife for the sum
         Five hundred & twenty pounds current money of Virginia to them in hand paid
they do hereby grant unto the said Zachariah Sims 60 acres and a half Begining at two
red oaks in MICHAEL RUSSELLs line one of which is dead thence with his line South to
one white oak Corner to said Russell and GEORGE RAISOR thence South Raisors line to
two Maples on Little Dark Run North to a red oak on the said Run at the mouth of the
Spring Branch thence up the several courses of sd run north opisit the Spring the
same courses continued to Russells line thence with the said line to the begining containing 52 acres Also one other tract of land bought of Conrad Delph and Mary his Wife
Begining at three Maples in a branch thence South thence down the branch to the
begining containing 80 acres and a half the said Ephraim Klugh & Conrad Delph and
Mary his Wife to hold the sd 60 acres & a half unto said Zachariah Sims . . . .
In presents of us WILLIAM POWELL,   Conrad ✳ Delph
         MICHAEL CLORE, MICHAEL SWINDLE   Anneymade ⅄ Delph
                                                              Ephraim Klugh

At a Court held for Culpeper County the 16th of August 1779
This Indenture ordered to be recorded.

pp.   On margin: D D to DEAR Oct 5th 1784
395-   THIS INDENTURE made the Twenty sixth day of July 1779 Betwen JOHN WAYLAND
398   and CATHARINE his Wife of the County of Culpeper of one part & JOHN DEER
      JUNR. of County aforesaid Witnesseth that said John Wayland and Catharine his
Wife for sum of Eighty pounds current money of Virginia do hereby grant unto the said
John Deer junr. his heirs Eighty eight and a half acres of land in Culpeper County and
Bromfield Parish in the Robinson Fork of Rappadan River bounded Begining at GEORGE
LAYMANs Corner & Runs thence South to two pines thence East to the begining place ..
In Presents of us JAMES BARBOUR,   John X Wayland
      JAMES BARBOUR JUNR., WILLIAM WALKER,   Catharine x Wayland
      MORDICAI BARBOUR
  THE COMMONWEALTH of Virginia to JAMES BARBOUR & WILLIAM WALKER Gent Where-
as John Wayland and Catharine his Wife have sold land in the County of Culpeper unto
John Deer junr. and Whereas the said Catharine cannot travel to our County Court to
make acknowledgement of the said conveyance we do give you power to go to the said
Katharine and examine her prively from her husband whether she doth the same
freely and when you have received her acknowledgement that you Certify us thereof
in our said Court. Witness JOHN JAMESON Clerk of our said Court the 26th of July 1779 in
the Fourth year of the Commonwealth.
  By virtue of the within Commission we did go to the said Catharine and did examine
her apart from her husband touching the ackowledgement of the Conveyance & she
declared she did the same freely and was willing the same be recorded in the County
Court of Culpeper. Given this 26th day of July 1779.
              JAMES BARBOUR   WILLIAM WALKER
At a Court held for Culpeper County the 16th of August 1779
This Indenture with the Commission & Certificate is ordered to be recorded.

pp.   On margin: D D J DAY 95
398-   We WILLIAM DAY, CASSOM DAY, CHARLES DAY, HENRY DAY, JOHN COLVIN and
399   CHARLES COLVIN are firmly bound under JOHN DAY in sum of Ten thousand
      pounds current money of Virginia payment to be made to said John Day dated
this 22nd day of June 1779.
  Whereas the above bound (names repeated) were intitled to an equal share or divident
of the Estate of FRANCES DAY decd and did mutually agree to, and apoint said John Day to
act for the whole of them in selling the Estate of the said Decedent & whereas John Day
was Obliged (as acting person) to give bills of sales & other indemnities to the percha-
sers of said Estate Now if the said (names repeated) their heirs do stand to, and indem-
nify John Day in all his proceedings as actor, for the whole and do pay an Equal part of
all or any Damages which may be recovered of said John Day for his acting aforesaid
then this Obligation to be void Else to remain in full force against the Delinquent or De-
linquents only and their heirs.
In presents of D. JAMESON JUNR.,   William Day   Henry Day
      RICHD. YOUNG   Cassam Day   John Colvin
                               Charles Day   Charles Colvin
At a Court held for Culpeper County the 16th of August 1779
This Bond ordered to be recorded.

pp.   On margin: D D   R. SMITH Son of JOSEPH 97
400-   THIS INDENTURE made the 16th day of August 1779 Between AMBROSE MEDLEY
404   and FRANCES his Wife of Parish of Brumfield and County of Culpeper of one part
        and JOSEPH SMITH of Parish and County aforesaid Witnesseth that said Ambrose
Medley and Francis his Wife for sum Two hundred and twenty six pounds Fifteen shillings and seven pence half penney current money of Virginia hath sold unto said
Joseph Smith his heirs One hundred and two and one half acres of land in the Parish
and County aforesaid and bounded begining at two red oaks Corner to BENJAMIN FIN-
NELL thence North to a white oak Corner to said Benjamin Finnell in THOMAS SHELTONs
line thence with Sheltons line South West to a Spanish oak Corner to said Thomas Shelton thence South to two posts Oaks Corner to FRANCIS GIBBS thence North to a Chusnut
stake in Orchard thence North East to a hickory in Francis Gibbs line thence South to
the Begining . . . .

                                                                Ambrose Medley
    At a Court held for Culpeper County the 16th day of August 1779
This Indenture and Memorandum ordered to be recorded on the motion of the said
Joseph Smith a dedimus is awarded for the private examination of said Frances which
when returned with the Certificate thereon is ordered to be recorded.
THE COMMONWEALTH OF VIRGINIA to Gent. Greeting Whereas Ambrose Medley and
Frances his Wife have sold land in County of Culpeper to Joseph Smith and Whereas the
said Frances cannot travel to our County Court of Culpeper to make acknowledgement of
the said conveyance we do give you power to personally go to the said Frances and examine her apart from her husband whether she doth the same freely and when you
have received her acknowledgement that you Certifie us thereof in our said Court.
Witness JOHN JAMESON Clerk the 16th day of August 1779 & fourth year of the Commonwealth.

pp.   THIS INDENTURE made the first day of April 1771 Betwen AMBROSE MEDLEY of
404-   Parish of Brumfield in County of Culpeper and FRANKEY his Wife of one part
407   and FRANCIS GIBBS of Parish and County aforesaid Witnesseth that Ambrose
        Medley and Frankey his Wife for sum Twenty three pounds Two and sixpence
current money of Virginia hath granted unto the said Francis Gibbs his heirs forever
land in the Parish and County aforesaid and being part of land that BENJAMIN FINNELL
perchased of Ambrose Medley containing ten acres and a half bounded Begining at two
box oaks in Francis Gibbs line thence South to a nother stake in the Orchard thence
West to two red oaks in Francis Gibbses line . . . .

                                                                Ambrose Medley
THE COMMONWEALTH OF VIRGINIA Gent. Whereas AMBROSE MEDLEY and FRANCIS his
Wife have sold to Francis Gibbs land in the County of Culpeper and Whereas the said
Frances cannot travil to our said Court of Culpeper to make acknowledgment of the said
conveyance we do give you power to go to the said Francis and examine her apart from
her husband whether she doth the same freely and is willing same shall be recorded in
our County Court and when you have examined her as aforesaid that you Certifie us
thereof in our said Court. Witness JOHN JAMESON Clerk the 16th of August 1779 and
fourth year of the Commonwealth.
    At a Court held for Culpeper County the 16th of August 1779
This Indenture with the Memorandum thereon and a Commission award for the private
Examination of said Frankey which when returned with Certificate is also ordered to be
recorded.

pp.   THIS INDENTURE made this 16th of August 1779 Betwen AMBROSE MEDLEY and
407-   FRANCES his Wife of Parish of Brumfield and County of Culpeper of one part and
410   BENJAMIN FINNELL of Parish and County aforesaid Witnesseth that said Ambrose
        Medley and Frances his Wife for sum of Two hundred and fifty pounds of good
and Lawfull money of Virginia hath granted unto Benjamin Fennell his heirs One hundred and thirteen acres of land in the Parish and County aforesaid and bounded begining at a pine South to CHARLES BROOKING line thence South to the begining . . . .
                                                                    Ambrose Medley
    At a Court held for Culpeper County the 16th of Augt 1779
This Indenture with Memorandum and a Commission awarded for the private Examination of said Frankey which when returned is also ordered to be recorded.

pp.   On margin: D D to WILLIAM McQUEEN Aug 1780
411-   TO ALL TO WHOM Know ye that I ALEXANDER McQUEEN JUNR. of Culpeper County
412   for natual love which I do bear to my Brother WILLIAM McQUEEN of said County
        and for Five shillings current money of Virginia I do grant to the said William
McQueen his heirs one negroe boy named Jim which said Negroe boy Jim I do hereby
warrant against clame of any person. In Witness whereof I have set my hand and seal
this 14th day of August 1779.
                                                                    Alexander McQueen
    At a Court held for Culpeper County the 16th of August 1779
This Indenture Deed of Gift ordered to be recorded.

pp.   THIS INDENTURE made the 23rd day of August 1779 Betwen BENJAMIN LILLARD
412-   of County of Culpeper and his Wife of one part and WILLIAM CHAMPE of afore-
415   said County Witnesseth that said Benjamin Lillard and FRANKEY his Wife for
        sum of Seven hundred and fifty pounds current money to said Benjamin Lillard
in hand paid by said William Champe have granted unto said William Champe his heirs
land in County of Culpeper and Parish of Brumfield on the North side of Pophams Run
containing Twenty acres & three quarters of an acre according to a Servey made by Mr.
JAMES GRAVES bounded Begining at four Willows near the bank of the aforesaid
Pophams Run Corner to aforesaid Champe and runs thence with his line North West to
the MAIN ROAD thence up the several courses of the said road as South West to the
aforesaid Run thence down the said run South from thence to the begining . . . .
Presents of WILLIAM BROWN,   Benjamin Lillard
        JOHN SLAUGHTER, B. NELSON,   Frankey Lillard
        AARON BEREY
THE COMMONWEALTH OF VIRGINIA to WILLIAM BROWN, JOHN SLAUGHTER and GEORGE
WETHERALL Gent Whereas Benjamin Lillard and Frankey his Wife have conveyed land
in County of Culpeper on the North side of Pophams Run to William Champe & Whereas
the said Frankey cannot travil to our County Court of Culpeper to make acknowledgement of the said conveyance we do give you power to go to the said Frankey and
examine her apart from her husband whether she doth the same freely and when you
have received her acknowledgement that you Certifie us thereof in our said Court. Witness JOHN JAMESON Clerk of our said Court this 23d of August 1779 and in the third year
of the Commonwealth.
    By virtue of the within Commission we did go to the within named Frankey Lillard and
she did acknowledge that she without the threates of her husband did desire that the
annexed Deed should be recorded in Court of Culpeper Witness this 23d day of August
1779.   WILLIAM BROWN   JOHN SLAUGHTER

At a Court held for Culpeper County the 20th day of Sept. 1779
This Indenture with Receipt and a Commission thereto annexed and Certificate &
ordered to be recorded.

pp.   THIS INDENTURE made the tenth day of February 1775 Betwen PETER RUCKER
415- and SARAH his Wife of Parish of Bromfield and County of Culpeper of one part
417   and MICHAEL EHART of the Parish and County aforesaid Witnesseth that said
      Peter Rucker and Sarah his Wife for sum of Forty five pounds current money of
Virginia hath granted unto the said Michael Ehart his heirs forever land in the County
of Culpeper and being part of the land granted by Lord THOMAS FAIRFAX 1754 whereon
JACOB HUBBAR now liveth containing One hundred and eighty one acres of land and
bounded by the lands of Messrs. JOSEPH HENDERSON, JAMES ALEXANDER, JOSEPH
RUCKER, GEORGE RUCKER and MICHAEL EHART . . . .
In Presents of us WILLIAM WALKER,   Peter Rucker
     JOHN GIBBS, JONATHAN UNDERWOOD,   Sarah Rucker
     JAMES FINNEL, GEORGE WAYL
   At a Court held for Culpeper County the 15th day of May 1775
This Indenture from Peter Rucker & Sarah his Wife ordered to be recorded And at a
Court held for the said County the 20th day of September 1779 was fully proved and
ordered to be recorded.

pp.   THIS INDENTURE made this 20th of September 1779 Betwen MATTHIAS MOCK and
417- his Wife BARBARY of County of Culpeper of one part and FISHER RICE of afore-
420   said County Witnesseth that for the sum Fifty pounds current money of Virginia
      the said Matthias Mock and Barbary his Wife hath granted unto said Fisher Rice
his heirs forever land in County of Culpeper containing Twenty five acres and bound
begining at a poplar in said Mocks line thence with his line South to red oaks in COOKs
line thence with his line to Mocks old line thence with his line to the beging . . . .
In presents of us JOHN FINKS,   Matthias Mocks
     MARK FINKS, ANDREW FINKS   Barbary Mocks
   At a Court held for Culpeper County the 20th of Sept 1779
This Indenture ordered to be recorded.

pp.   THIS INDENTURE made this Twentieth day Spt. in the year 1779 Betwen FISHER
420- RICE and AGNESS his Wife of County of Culpeper of one part and MATTHIAS MOCK
422   of County of Culpeper Witnesseth that for sum of Five pounds current money of
      Virginia to Fisher Rice whereof I do hereby acknowledge and by these presents
the said Fisher Rice and Agnes his wife hath granted unto Matthias Mock his heirs forever land in the County of Culpeper containing Twelve acres and a half more or less
bounded Begining at three white oaks standing in Fisher Rices line thence with Rices
line North to said Mocks old line thence with his line to the beginning . . . .
                                                             Fisher Rice
   At a Court held for Culpeper County the 20th day of Sept 1779
This Indenture and receipt ordered to be recorded.

pp.   THIS DEED OF FEEOFFMENT made September the 18th day 1779 Betwen WILLIAM
422- MORRISS and ELIZABETH his Wife of Culpeper County of one part and JOSHUA
425   MORRISS of same County Witnesseth that said William Morriss and Elizabeth his
      Wife for sum of one hundred pounds lawfull money of Virginia William Morriss
and Elizabeth his wife hath granted unto said Joshua Morris his heirs forever land in
County aforesaid and being part of a tract of Four hundred and three acres granted to

JOHN WILHOIT by the right Honourable THOMAS LORD FAIR FAX by Deed dated the 16th
day of November 1756 Registered in the Proprietors Office in Book H Folio 738 Begining
at a small branch at two white oaks East up the said branch to a line of JOHN STROTHERs
thence South down said Strothers line to a poplar Corner to said Strother tract thence
down said Strothers line to the place of begining containing one hundred acres ....

William Morris
Elizabeth Morris

At a Court held for Culpeper County the 20th of
September 1779 This Indenture ordered to be recorded
the said Elizabeth being previly examined according to Law.

pp.   On margin: D D 1792
425-   THIS INDENTURE made the 30th of August 1779 Betwen JOSEPH EARLY and JANE
429   his Wife and ADAM GAAR of County of Culpeper of one part and JAMES BARBOUR
          of said County of other part Witnesseth that said Joseph Early & Jane his Wife
Adam Gaar for the sum Fourteen hundred pounds current money of Virginia by said
James Barbour paid have each of them granted unto said James Barbour his heirs forever Five hundred and forty acres of land in the County of Culpeper bounded Begining
at a white hickory on the White Oak Run Corner with ADAM CHRISTLER thence with his
line North to a red oak Corner with JOHN BERRY thence with his lines North to two
white oaks Corner with said Berry and JACOB BROYLE near a branch thence with
Broyles line South to a red oak in a Valey thence down the Valley to the Spring thence
down the Spring Branch to the White Oak Run thence crossing the said White Oak Run
to three red oaks Corner to MARTIN ROUSE thence with Rouses line so as to include forty
eight acres of the said Rouses land thence down a direct line from Rouses line to the
White Oak Run thence up the White Oak Run to the begining ....

In presents of us JOEL EARLY,   Joseph Early
      ELIJAH KIRTLEY, EPHM. RUCKER,   Jane Early
      JOHN YAGER, JOHN BREEDLOVE,   Adam Gaar
      JOHN FINNEY, JOHN ✗ WAYLAND,
      RICHARD ✛ TARRELL
At a Court held for Culpeper County the 20th of September 1779
This Indenture was proved as to Joseph Early & Adam Gaar and acknowledged by LEWIS
GAAR and ordered to be recorded.

pp.   THIS INDENTURE made the Fourth day of August 1779 Betwen THOMAS WALL and
429-   MARY his Wife of County of Culpeper of one part and JOHN ERHARDT OELSHLA-
431   GEL of same County Clothier Witnesseth that for sum One hundred pounds cur-
          rent money of Virginia paid by said JOHN ERHARDT said Thomas Wall and Mary
his Wife do hereby grant unto said John Erhardt his heirs land devised to a certain
JOSEPH HOLTZCLAW and to MARY the Wife of DANNIEL BENNIT by JOHN HOLTZCLAW
Deceased their Fathers last Will and Testament being two thirds of a tract of land in
Culpeper County by Deed from the Proprietors Office dated the 5th day of March 1753
containing Nine hundred and eighty seven acres the said Deed having issued out in the
name of HENRY, JOSEPH and MARY HOLTZCLAW, the Sons and Daughter of JOHN HOLTZ-
CLAW deceased the said two thirds part containing by Estimation Six hundred and fifty
eight acres leaving behind untouched the other third devised to HENRY HOLTZCLAW ...
In presents of us ANTHONY FOSTER,   Thomas Wall
      ROBERT COLEMAN JUR., HENRY MILLER   Mary Wall
At a Court held for Culpeper County the 20th day of September 1779
This Indenture ordered to be recorded.

pp.   THIS INDENTURE made this 20th day of September 1779 Betwen CHARLES SPIL-
431-   MAN and ELIZABETH his Wife of County of Culpeper of one part and WILLIAM
432   MITCHELL of County of STAFFORD Witnesseth that said Charles Spilman and Eliza-
         beth his Wife for sum Six hundred pounds in hand paid have granted unto said
William Mitchell his heirs Two hundred acres of land bounded begining at a chusnut
and white oak Corner ABSOLUMS ADAMS and runing with his line North East near the
head of a branch to a Chesnut on the North River thence up the river the several
courses to a white oak Corner to WILLIAM RUSSELL Gent. by the mouth of a branch
thence South to a white oak Markt W R on the South side of a branch being a Corner to
William Russell and THOMPSON with or near Thompsons line North to the land of said
Thompson thence to the begining . . . .

                                                                   Charles Spilman
     At a Court held for Culpeper County the 20th of September   Elizabeth Spilman
1779 This Indenture ordered to be recorded the said Elizabeth
being privily examined according to Law.

pp.   On margin: D D   D. FIELD jr 1805
432-   THIS INDENTURE made this Twentieth day of September 1779 Betwen GEORGE
434   DOGGETT of County of Culpeper of one part and THOMAS BROWN of aforesaid
         County Witnesseth that said George Doggett for sum One hundred and seventy
three pounds Fifteen shillings current money of Virginia paid by said Thomas Brown
he doth grant unto said Thomas Brown land in County of Culpeper containing Two hundred acres which said tract of land is part of a tract of Five hundred and seventy five
acres granted to ANDREW BROWN as by Patent from the Proprietors Office bearing date
the 11th day of June 1749, and by him conveyed to said George Doggett and bounded
Begining at three pines Corner to a tract first surveyed for WILLIAM TAPP and runing
North to a persimmon on Easthams Run thence South to a pine near a ROAD thence
South to the begining . . . .

                                                                   George Doggett
     At a Court held for Culpeper County the 20th of September 1779
This Indenture ordered to be recorded.

pp.   On margin: D D 1790
434-   THIS INDENTURE made this 20th of September 1779 Betwen JOHN MINOR and
436   MARY his Wife of County of Culpeper of one part and THOMAS CAUN of afore-
         said County and Parish Witnesseth that said John Minor and Mary his Wife for
sum Three thousand seven hundred pounds current money of Virginia paid by Thomas
Caun doth grant unto Thomas Caun his heirs for ever land in the aforesaid County
containing Five hundred and six acres and bounded Begining at three chesnut trees on
an arm of POES MOUNTAIN the South side of said Mountain runing South to a Spanish
oak near a Corner of John Minors fence and is a Corner in COURNS MITCHELLs line
thence North to a white oak a supposed Corner by the side of a branch near another
Corner of said Minor fence thence North to a pine Corner to JOSEPH ASBURYs thence
North to a pine Corner of RICHARD HARRIS's in Joseph Asburys line thence North to a
branch the South Fork of Hungry Run thence up the said branch dividing the land
from THORNTONs land (THOMPTONs marked out) to a Spanish Oak on the North side of
said branch thence continuing up the said branch to two white oaks a Corner of BEN-
JAMIN DOUGLAS's in the Fork of two branches thence up the right hand pronge to a
line of marked trees that devides this land from the land of Benjamin Douglas's thence
with line of marked trees to two red oaks on the East side of Poes Mountain thence cross

the said Mountain a strait line to the begining place . . . .

John Minor
Mary Minor

At a Court held for Culpeper County the 20th of Sept 1779
This Indenture and receipt ordered to be recorded the said
Mary being prevely examined according to Law.

pp.   On margin: Dd. RICHD. HARRIS 1804
437-   THIS INDENTURE made this 20th of September 1779 Betwen JOHN MINOR and
439   MARY his Wife of County of Culpeper and State of Virginia of one part and
        GEORGE HARRISS of County of MONGUMRY and State of MARYLAND Witnesseth
that John Minor and Mary his Wife for sum of Eighty pounds current money of Virginia paid by George Harriss do hereby sell unto said George Harriss land in County of
Culpeper containing One hundred and twenty acres which said tract of land is part of a
tract of One thousand acres granted to THOMAS MINOR by COLO. LEWIS the Day of 1771 as
by the Patent from the Proprietors Office may appear and bounded Begining at a
Spanish Oak Corner to MERRYMANS SETTLEs land and runing with his line North to a
pine on POUGHS ROAD thence up the said Road North to three white oaks on Hungry
Run thence up the said Run South to the Fork of the said Run thence up the South Fork
South to the Mouth of a branch thence leaving said Run South to a pine in a line of
JOSEPH ASHBURRYs land thence with said line East to the begining . . . .

John Minor
Mary Minor

At a Court held for Culpeper County the 20th of
September 1779 This Indenture and receipt ordered to be
recorded the said Mary being previly examined according to Law.

pp.   TO ALL PEOPLE I BENJAMIN GAINS of County of Culpeper and Bromfield Parish in
439-   Colony of Virginia sends Greeting Know ye that I Benjamin Gains for divers
440   good causes and in consideration of the love and Effection I bear unto my Son
        WILLIAM GAINS I have granted unto William Gains his heirs land takend of the
tract that I now live on containing sixty acres being in Culpeper County and Goardvine
Fork Bromfield Parish and bounded with the BAIRARSS MOUNTAIN in an old line thence
with said line North to a red oak near to a branch in a line of Mr. THOMPSONs thence
with said line North to a white oak on a branch side near a large Glade still a Corner to
Thompson thence South to the begining I do give the land unto William Gains in manner following Vizt. I reserve this part of the property that said Williams Gains shall not
sell or dispose of the said land during my natural life without my Consent & after my
death the said land and premises shall for ever hereafter remain unto said William
Gains. In Witness whereof I have set my hand and seal this Twentieth day of September
1779.

Benj. Gains

At a Court held for Culpeper County the 20th day of September 1779
This Indenture Deed of Gift ordered to be recorded.

pp.   THIS INDENTURE made this 26th day of July 1778 Betwen THOMAS MARSTIN of
440-   one part and THOMAS CLERK Son of JAMES CLERK Witnesseth that for Natual
441   love and affection which said Thomas Marstin hath unto said Thomas Clerk hath
        given one Certain negro girl named Sillah to hold the said negro girl and her
increase. In Witness whereof hath set his hand affixed his seal the day and year above
written.

Thomas Marstin

At a Court held for Culpeper County the 16th of November 1778
This Indenture was ordered to be recorded.

pp.   On margin: D D NALES CALVERT 1792
441-   THIS INDENTURE made this Fourth (inserted Fifteenth) day of February 1779
445   Betwen JOHN CALVERT and HELEN his Wife of County of BALTIMORE and Pro-
          vince of MARYLAND of one part and GEORGE CALVERT of County of Culpeper and
Colony of Virginia of the other part Witnesseth that said John Calvert and Helen his
Wife for sum One hundred and fifty pounds current money of Virginia hath granted
unto the said George Calvert his heirs land in County of Culpeper it being part of a
large tract of land of One thousand Nine hundred and thirty one acres granted to JOHN
FROGG and MICHAL WALLACE by Pattent dated the 27th of June 1751 and conveyed to
GEORGE CALVERT JUNR. by aforenamed JOHN CALBER by Deeds dated the 25th and 26th
days of March 1777 and conveyed to the aforenamed John Calvert by the aforenamed
George Calvert Junr. by Deed dated the Twenty third day of June 1778 containing three
hundred and seventeen acres of land and bounded Begining at three red oaks corner to
the above mentioned Patent thence with the Patent line North to a small chesnut tree
on the side of a Mountain thence North to three dogwoods on a branch thence North to
three hickories near VASES arm thence South East leaving the Patent line South to
McCLANAHANs line thence North to the begining . . . .
In the presents of us THOMAS McCLANAHAN,   John Calvert
          JAMES BROWNING, JOHN BRADFORD,   Hellen Calvert
          JOHN STROTHER, JOHN SLAUGHTER
     (Witnesses on the Receipt): ARCHIBALD BIGBEE, CHAS. STEWARD, JOHN CALVERT
THE COMMONWEALTH OF VIRGINIA to JOHN STROTHER, WM. BROWN & JOHN SLAUGHTER
Gent Whereas John Calvert and Helen his Wife have conveyed land in Culpeper County
to George Calvert and whereas the said Helen cannot travil to our County Court of Culpeper to make acknowledgement of the said conveyance we give you power to go to the
said Helen and examine her apart from her husband whether she doth the same freely
and when you have received her acknowledgement that you certify us thereof in our
said Court. Witness JOHN JAMESON Clk of our Court the 15th day of February 1779.
     Culpeper SCT. By Virtue of the within Writ we caused the within named Helen Calvert
to come before us & Exd. her apart from her husband touching her acknowledgement of
the Deed who acknowledged the same & desired it might be recorded in the Court of
Culpeper. Witness this 1st day of March 1779.
                                   JOHN STROTHER   JOHN SLAUGHTER

pp.   On margin: D. D.. to Mr. DAVENPORT Apl. 82
445-   THIS INDENTURE made the 16th day of August 1779 Betwen JAMES HANSBUROUGH
448   SENR. of County of STAFFORD and LETTICE his Wife of one part and BIRKETT
          DAVENPORT of County of Culpeper Witnesseth that said James Hansbrough Senr.
and Lettice his Wife for sum of Thirteen hundred and two pounds current money of
Virginia paid by said Birkett Davenport he hath granted unto said Birkett Davenport his
heirs a tract of land purchased by him the said James Hansbrough of WILLIAM TUTT
and SARAH his Wife as will more fully appear by Deeds of Conveyance lodge in the
Secretaries Office at Williams burg lying in the Parish of St. Marks in the County of
Culpeper Begining at three white oaks Corner to JAMES WHITEHEAD in STROTHERs line
thence North to a white oak Corner in YANCEYs line thence South to two red oak saplins
in PARKERs line thence with Parkers line to Whiteheads Corner thence to the begining
containing Two hundred and Seventeen acres . . . .

In presents of us SAM CLAYTON JR.,   James Hansbrough
     PHILIP PENDLETON, ALEXANDER McQUEEN JUNR.,   Lettis Hansbrough
     JAMES WHITEHEAD
  At a Court held for Culpeper County the 20th day of Septr 1779
This Indenture with Memorandum and Receipt ordered to be recorded.

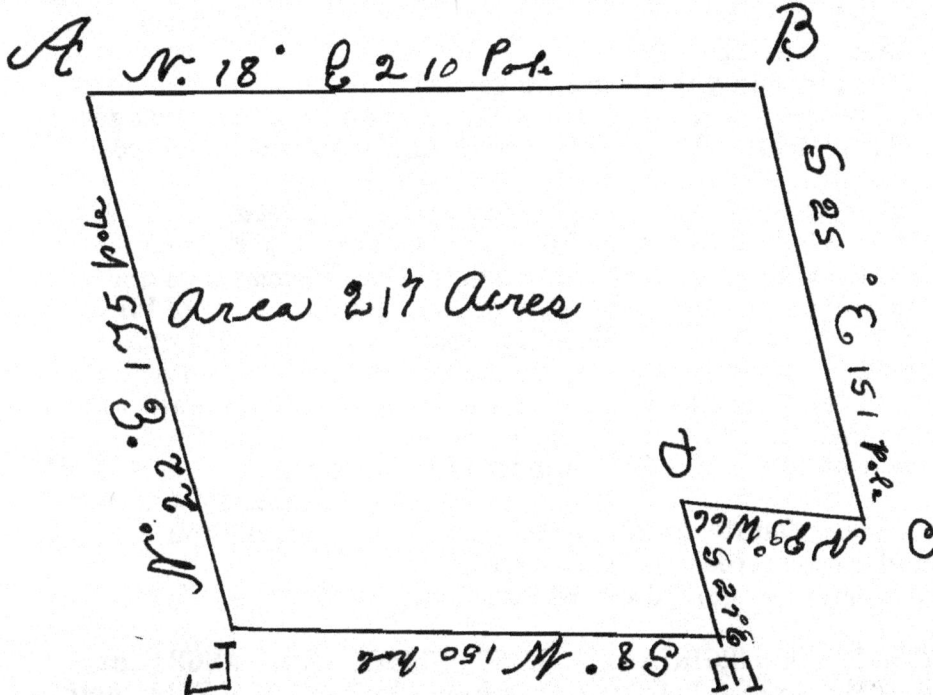

A   N. 18° E 210 Pole   B

S 25° E 151 Pole

N. 22° E 175 Pole

area 217 acres

N 9° W 66

S 27° E

D

S 8° W 150 Pole

E

C

pp.   On margin: D D JOS: EDDENS 1791
448-   THIS INDENTURE made the Twentyforth day of August 1778 Betwen RUBEN
450   UNDERWOOD of Parish of Saint Thomas and County of ORANGE of one part and
      THOMAS MAXWELL of Parish of Bromfield and County of Culpeper Witnesseth
that said Reuben Underwood for sum of Sixty pounds current money paid by said Thomas Maxwell hath granted unto said Thomas Maxwell his heirs forever land in the Parish and County aforesaid and in the Fork of the Conway and Stanton Rivers and containing One hundred acres, and is bounded by the lines of FRANCIS CONWAY, WILLIAM KIRLTLEY and JOHN DELANEY . . . .
In presents of us WILLIAM KIRTLEY,   Ruben Underwood
     EPHRAIM RUCKER, WILLIAM WALKER,
     GEORGE EVE
  At a Court held for Culpeper County the 21st of September 1778
This Indenture was partly proved and ordered to be Certified and at a Court held for the said County the 19th day of October 1778 was further proved and ordered to be certified and at a Court held for the said County the 21st day of September 1779 was fully proved and ordered to be recorded.

pp.   On margin: D D A. WHITE 1789
451-   THIS INDENTURE made the third day of April 1778 Betwen JAMES CRUMP of
453   County of FAIRFAX of one part and JOHN BARNHISSEL JUNOR of County of Cul-
      peper Witnesseth that said James Crump for sum of Forty pounds current money
of Virginia hath granted unto said John Barnhysle junor his heirs One hundred and eleven acres of land in Culpeper County and Bromfield Parish in the Goardvine Fork of

Rappahannock River joining the lines of the Revd. JOHN THOMSON Deceast and John Barnhysle junor and begining at a Chesnut tree Corner to John Barnhysle in said Thompsons line thence with Thompsons line to the said Barnhysle line on the top of the Mountain thence down an arm of the Mountain with said Barnhysles line to the begining . . . .

In presents of us RICHARD X VOAN,   James Crump
    LEROY HILL, SAMUEL HISLE

At a Court held for Culpeper County the 16th of November 1778 This Indenture was partly proved and ordered to be Certified And at a Court held for the said County the 20th of September 1779 was fully proved and ordered to be recorded.

pp.   THIS INDENTURE made the Twentieth day of September 1779 Between THOMAS
453-   COON and SARAH his Wife of County of Culpeper of one part and NALLEY MADDOX
454   of the same County of the other part Witnesseth that said Thomas Coon and Sarah
        his wife for sum of Two hundred and Eighty pounds current money of Virginia paid by said Nelley Maddox have sold unto said Nalley Maddox his heirs land situate near CHESNUT GAP and bounded Begining at a poplar on the Hedgman River thence South to a double white oak on the ROAD Corner to WETHERS thence South to three white oaks Corner to DIXON thence with his line North to three red oaks on the said river thence up the river to the begining containing Four hundred and seventy five acres of land . .

                                    Thomas Coon
At a Court held for Culpeper County the 20th of Sept 1779   Sarah Coon
This Indenture ordered to be recorded previous to which the said Sarah was first privily examined according to Law.

p.   THE COMMONWEALTH OF VIRGINIA to JAMES SLAUGHTER, JOHN WAUGH Gent
455   Whereas WILLIAM SPARKS & ELIZABETH his Wife & RICHARD SCALES by their
      certain Indenture of feoffment bearing date 8th of February 1779 have sold
unto JOSEPH PORTER the fee simple Estate of Five acres of land in the County of Culpeper and whereas Elizabeth cannot travel to our Court of Culpeper to make acknowledgement of the said conveyance we do give you power to receive the acknowledgement which the said Elizabeth shall be willing to make and when you have examined her as aforesaid that you Certify us thereof in our said Court. Witness JOHN JAMESON Clerk of our Court this 20th day of September 1779 and in the 4 year of the Commonwealth.

In Obedience to the within order we have personally taken the private examination of Elizabeth Sparks and she freely consents and that same shall be recorded in Court. Witness this 20th day of September 1779.
                 JAMES SLAUGHTER   JOHN WAUGH

pp.   On margin: D D WM. RICHARDS p order 1802
455-   THIS INDENTURE made the 26th of January 1779 Between ALEXANDER SPOTSWOOD
458   esquire and ELIZABETH his Wife of County of SPOTSYLVANIA of one part and
      SIMON MILLER of County of Culpeper Witnesseth that said Alexander Spotswood and Eliza. his Wife for Twelve hundred and fifty pounds Curt. money hath this day sold unto the said Simon Miller his heirs land in Culpeper County and bounded Begining on the South side of the North River at a Maple near a small Island thence along a line formerly run by RICHARD YOUNG near STANTONs now SLAUGHTERs line to a pine adjoining Mr. BOWLES ARMISTEADs line thence along the line by said Young Between Colo. Spotswood and Mr. Armistead down Gils Run to a Corner white oak being the Corner tree between CHARLES BENSON and COLO. JOHN SPOTSWOOD thence along the dividing line between said Benson and Spotswood to a Locust on the North River thence

up the river to the begining. And Whereas some doubts may arise from a claim that
might be made by MAJR. JOHN SPOTSWOOD his heirs or assigns in order to remove the
same the said John Spotswood and SARAH his Wife hath become parties to this present
Indenture confirming the same relinquishing all claim . . . .

In presence of B. JOHNSTON,   Alexander Spotswood
    WILLIAM RICHARDS, DANIEL JAMES   Elizabeth Spotswood
                                      John Spotswood
                                      Salley Spotswood

   Memo of an Agreement Between Alexander Spotswood and
Simon Miller the said Spotswoods sells unto said Miller Fifteen hundred acres of land on
the Rappahannock River called the North River but if on a Survey the said tract shall
be found to contain more land the overplus is to be allotted unto the said Alexander
Spotswood where it shall be the least prejudicial to the said Miller and in case it should
not contain Fifteen hundred acres of land that what is wanting shall be made up out of
any land the said Spotswood may have claim or own adjoining the same but in case said
Spotswood has no land adjoining that then the said Simon Miller is never to have any
claim against the said Alexander Spotswood his heirs for such a deficiency. In Witness
whereof the parties hath set their hand . . . .

Witness present B. JOHNSTON,   A. Spotswood
    WM. RICHARD, DANIEL JAMES

  At a Court held for Culpeper County the 17th of May 1779
This Indenture from Alexander Spotswood and Elizabeth his Wife and John Spotswood
and Sally his Wife was partly proved by the Oath of Benjamin Johnston a witness which
was ordered to be C and at a Court held the 21st day of June 1779 was further proved by
the Oaths of William Richards and Daniel James and ordered to be recorded.

END   JOHN JAMESON CCC

ADAMS. Absolum 72; Charles 25.

ADKINS. Ambrose 58.

ALBETT. Daniel 61.

ALCOCK. Robert 7, 8, 32, 60.

ALEXANDER. James 70.

ALLEN. Line of 64; Thomas 17;
 William 19, 33.

AMERICAN FREE STATES 40.

ARMISTEAD. Bowles 76.

ARNOLD. James 15.

ASBURY. Joseph 72, 73.

ASHBY. George 32.

AYLOR (ALER). Henry 64; Margaret 64, 65.

BACK. John 65; Margaret 65.

BACKER. Henry 51, 52.

BAKER. David 33.

BALL. William 38.

BALLENGER. Darcus 20; James 20.

BANKS. Adam 14, 45; Ann 25;
 Gerrard 25, 44, 45; Richard 33; Tunstal 53.

BARBOUR. Colo. 54; James 5, 10, 31, 48, 49,
 67, 71; James Junr. 67; Mordecai 67;
 Thomas 7, 8, 9.

BARLER. Adam 49; Jacob 49.

BARNES. Leonard 7, 38, 55, 58;
 Sarah 58, 59.

BARNETT. Ambrose 4; John 31.

BARNHISLE. Frances 19; John 19, 76;
 John Junr. 75, 76.

BARRCILES. John 20.

BATTAILE. Nicholas 12, 37.

BAXTER. Alexander 33, 40; Mary 33.

BEALE. Line of 4; Taverner 60.

BEAZLEY. William 31.

BELL. James 55, 56; John M. 8;
 William 8.

BENNIT. Daniel 71; Mary (Holtzclaw) 71.

BENSON. Charles 44, 53, 76; Henry 44;
 John 44; Judith 44.

BERRY. Aaron 69; Acrey 12; Anthony 12;
 Jemima 2, 57, 58; John 2, 57, 58, 71.

BEVERLEY. Robert 44.

BIGBEE. Archibald 41, 74.

BISHOP. Jonathan 63; Line of 55; Mr. 63.

BLEDSOE. John 50; William 50, 51.

BLOODWORTH. Line of 26.

BLUNT. Charles 30; Francis 48.

BOBO. Absolom 3, 26; Line of 4.

BOHANNON. Am. 12; Ambrose 40, 53; Ann 53;
 Betty 31; Eliot Senr. 31, 53; John 53;
 Line of 54; Richard 31.

BOGLE. Merchant 43.

BOHAM. Thomas 53.

BOUGHAN. Mordecai 5; Vincent 5.

BOURN. Andrew 10; Jane 10.

BOWMER. William 15, 45.

BOYER. John 27.

BRADFORD. John 38, 74.

BRADLEY. John 20, 60; William 5, 46.

BRANHAM. Lott 1.

BREEDLOVE. John 47, 48.

BREFOARD. John 49.

BRENT. William 25, 26.

BRIDGE: Hungry Run 8.

BROOKING. Charles 69; Line of 50.

BROOKS. Suky 41; William 41.

BROWN. Ambrose 5; Andrew 72; Daniel 46;
 John 61; Line of 46; Thomas 28, 33, 66, 72;
 William 27, 28, 38, 39, 57, 69, 74;
 William C. 5, 28, 52; William Covington 52.

BROWNING. Charles 43; Edmond 24, 43;
 Francis 21; James 3, 38, 74; Joshua 13, 14;
 Mary 24; Susanna (Hickman) 3.

BROYLE. Adam 28; Delilah 12; Eve 28;
 Jacob 12, 71; John 12; Margaret 12; Mary 28;
 Matthias 28; Michael 28; Moses 5; Peter 12;
 Zackarias 12.

BRUCE. Alexander 36; Charles 26.

BUMGARDNER. George 18.

BURBRIDGE. Ben 11; Moses 51.

BURDINE. Ann 43; Line of 12; Reginal 19, 43, 61
 Nathaniel 10.

BURK. Alexander 13.

BURRELL. James 48.

BURTON. May 31.

BUTLER. John 25; Thomas 24; William 24.

BUTTON. John 27; Susannah 27; William 27.

CALVERT. George 38, 43, 74; George Jr. 3, 29,
 33, 38, 40, 43, 74; Helen 74; John 38, 74;
 Lydia B. 38; Nales 74.

CAMP. Ambrose 16; Henry 54; John 8, 54.

CAMPBELL. Isaac 3; Lucey 29, 30;
 Owen 24, 25; William 24.

CARPENTER. Andrew 49; Line of 63.

CARSEY. Samuel 37.

CARTER. Charles 4, 44, 59; George 55, 56;
 Line of 33; Salley 55, 56.

SERGANT. Line of 61.

SETTLE. Merryman 73.

SHEARWOOD. Line of 43.

SHELTON. Line of 15; Thomas 68.

SHOEMAKER. Abraham 63.

SHORTER. Henry 45.

SHOTWELL. Hannah 30;
Robert 19, 21, 22, 30.

SIMMS. Elijah 18; James 30; William 45;
Zachariah 66.

SKENKER. John 59.

SKREEN. Line of 32.

SLAUGHTER. Cadwallader 28; James 26, 58,
76; James Jr. 54; John 2, 5, 6, 28, 35, 36,
38, 39, 42, 43, 44, 51, 52, 57, 69, 74;
Line of 76; Ph. 39; Robert 54; Thomas 11.

SMITH. A. M. 61, 62; Benjamin 14; Dowg. 14;
Isaac 14, 15; John 49; Joseph 68;
Mallinder 15; R. 68; William 15.

SMOOT. Ben 38.

SNITHERS. Henry 43.

SPARKS. Elizabeth 26, 76; William 26, 76.

SPILMAN. Charles 72; Elizabeth 72.

SPOTSWOOD. Alexander 1, 11, 76, 77;
Ann 1; Deed 22; Elizabeth 76, 77;
John 1, 23, 64, 76, 77; Line of 26, 46;
Mary 1; Sarah 77.

STANTON. Line of 76; Thomas 25;
Will 14.

STARR. Jasper 3.

STATES: Delaware 25; Maryland 38, 73, 74;
North Carolina 24, 27; Pennsylvania 25;
West New Jersey 63.

STEVENS. Line of 16; Edward 46.

STEWARD. Charles 33, 41, 74; Daniel 41;
William 35.

STINNETT. Benjamin 19.

STONE. John 50.

STONEHOUSE. Line of 5.

STRODE. J. 55, 58; John 49.

STROTHER. French 8, 59; John 5, 6, 20, 34,
38, 42, 43, 44, 48, 51, 52, 71, 74; John
Jr. 34, 51, 52; Line of 74; Mary 6;
Robert 41, 42, 43, 51; William 12.

SWINDLE. Elizabeth 62; George 26;
Michael 62, 63, 66; Timothy 62.

TANNER. Christopher 64; Elizabeth 64;
Frederick 64.

TAPP. William 72.

TAYLOR. Argyle 32.

TEBBS. Faushee 32.

TERRILL (TARRELL). Edmund 66; John 7, 32;
Richard 71; Robert Jr. 7.

THOMAS. James 17; Jason 37; Mark 59;
Richard 13, 14; Rowland 7, 8, 9,. 65.

THOMPSON. John 56, 76; Line of 72, 73;
Waddy 14; William 1; William S. 1.

THORNTON. Ann 56, 57; Charles 32, 33;
Colo. 60; Francis 56; George 5, 8, 41, 42, 56,
57; John 5, 42; Line of 3, 72; Mary 5, 41, 42;
Presley 20, 21; Thomas 56; William 56, 59.

THRELKELD. Benjamin 20; John 20; Line of 55;
Moses 16; Nelly 16; Thomas 16.

TINSLEY. Edward 65.

TOMLIN(S). Martha 21, 22.

TOWLES. John 23.

TOWNS: Dumfries 25.

TRIPLETT. G. 33; John 32; William 48.

TURNER. Edward 10.

TURNLEY. Francis 35.

TUTT. James 41; John 31; Line of 27;
Sarah 74; William 74.

TWYMAN. Line of 50; William 39;
Winnefred 39.

TYLER. Henry 4, 29.

UNDERWOOD. Jonathan 70; Ruben 75.

VASS (VAUS). Edward 26, 58; Jean 26.

VAWTER. Jesse 47; Russell 47, 48.

VERNON. Mill 15; Richard 16, 55.

VISCARVER. Harmon 17.

VOAN. Richard 76.

VOSS. Edward 1, 2.

WALK. Martin 44.

WALKER. James 7, 8, 15; John 8, 42, 43, 51;
William 6, 7, 8, 67, 70, 75.

WALL. Mary 71; Thomas 71.

WALLACE. Michael 38, 74.

WALLIS. Behethelan 49; John 38, 49.

WARD. Ann 57; William 57.

WASHBORN. John 43.

WASHINGTON. Charles 59.

WATERFIELD. Phillip 24, 25.

WATKINS. Capt. 8; Edward 1.

WAUGH. Alexander 7, 31; Deed 22; John 17,
22, 23, 26, 76; Richard 58, 59.

WAYL. George 70.

WAYLAND. Catharine 67; John 28, 39, 54, 67, 71.
WEAVER. Peter 18; Philip 48; Tilman 27.
WEST. Edward 44; Edward Jr. 44.
WETHERALL. Ann 30; George 2, 11, 16, 19, 21, 22, 29, 30, 39, 42, 51, 52, 53, 69; Mary 30.
WHITE. A. 75; Abbott 29; Ann 23; Armistead 29; Daniel 22; James 29, 30; Margaret 30.
WHITEHEAD. James 25, 63, 74, 75.
WHITMORE (WHEETMORE). Ann 24, 25; Jacob 24, 25.
WIGINTON. John 11, 25, 36, 37, 43, 45, 46.
WILEY. Allen 12; George 21; John 21.
WILHOIT. Adam 23; Batey 23; Conrite 12; George 29, 49; John 71; Line of 28; Tobias 44.
WILLIAMS. Evan 25; James 20; John Jr. 22, 23.
WILLIS. Ann 23; Henry 13; James 22, 23; John 22, 23; Joseph 64; Joshua 10, 60, 64; Lewis 59; Sarah 22, 60; Survey 15.
WILSON. James 59; John 39; Lydia 59.
WIRT. George 25.

WOOD. Elizabeth 16; James 16; John Scott 16; Joseph 8, 10, 16, 24, 31, 32; Joseph Jr. 32, 49, 60; Judith 16; Mary 16.
WRIGHT. Hannah 17; Line of 66; Obediah 10, 17; Robert 33; William 4.

YAGER. John 71.
YANCEY. John 4, 29; Line of 16, 74; Phileman 25.
YARBROUGH. Ambrose 40; Mary 40.
YATES. Thomas 28, 52, 53.
YEAGER (YEGGER). Adam 5, 54; Adam Jr. 5; John 28, 49.
YOUNG. Line of 1; Richard 67, 76.
YOWELL. (YAWELL). David 21, 22, 39; Henry 40; James 20, 21, 22, 39; R. 61, 62.

ZACHARY. Ann 51; Benjamin 48, 51; Frankey 48; John 51; John Junr. 51; William 6, 29.
ZIGLAR. Christopher 52, 53.
ZIMMERMAN. Christopher 41, 53; Frederick 33; John Junr. 41; Katherine 41; Line of 59; Michael 41; Rubin 33; Sarah 33.

Heritage Books by Ruth and Sam Sparacio:

Abstracts of Account Books of Edward Dixon, Merchant of Port Royal, Virginia, Volume I. 1743–1747

Abstracts of Account Books of Edward Dixon, Merchant of Port Royal, Virginia, Volume II

Albemarle County, Virginia Deed and Will Book Abstracts, 1748–1752

Albemarle County, Virginia Deed Book Abstracts, 1758–1761

Albemarle County, Virginia Deed Book Abstracts, 1761–1764

Albemarle County, Virginia Deed Book Abstracts, 1764–1768

Albemarle County, Virginia Deed Book Abstracts, 1768–1770

Albemarle County, Virginia Deed Book Abstracts, 1776–1778

Albemarle County, Virginia Deed Book Abstracts, 1778–1780

Albemarle County, Virginia Deed Book Abstracts, 1780–1783

Albemarle County, Virginia Deed Book Abstracts, 1787–1790

Albemarle County, Virginia Deed Book Abstracts, 1790–1791

Albemarle County, Virginia Deed Book Abstracts, 1791–1793

Augusta County, Virginia Land Tax Books, 1782–1788

Augusta County, Virginia Land Tax Books, 1788–1790

Amherst County, Virginia Land Tax Books, 1789–1791

Caroline County, Virginia Appeals and Land Causes, 1787–1794

Caroline County, Virginia Committee of Safety and Early Surveys, 1729–1762 and 1774–1775

Caroline County, Virginia Land Tax Book Alterations, 1782–1789

Caroline County, Virginia Land Tax Book Alterations, 1792–1795

Caroline County, Virginia Land Tax Book Alterations, 1795–1798

Caroline County, Virginia Order Book Abstracts, 1765

Caroline County, Virginia Order Book Abstracts, 1767–1768

Caroline County, Virginia Order Book Abstracts, 1768–1770

Caroline County, Virginia Order Book Abstracts, 1770–1771

Caroline County, Virginia Order Book, 1764

Caroline County, Virginia Order Book, 1765–1767

Caroline County, Virginia Order Book, 1771–1772

Caroline County, Virginia Order Book, 1772–1773

Caroline County, Virginia Order Book, 1773

Caroline County, Virginia Order Book, 1773–1774

Caroline County, Virginia Order Book, 1774–1778

Caroline County, Virginia Order Book, 1778–1781

Caroline County, Virginia Order Book, 1781–1783

Caroline County, Virginia Order Book, 1783–1784

Caroline County, Virginia Order Book, 1784–1785

Caroline County, Virginia Order Book, 1785–1786

Caroline County, Virginia Order Book, 1786–1787

Caroline County, Virginia Order Book, 1787, Part 1

Caroline County, Virginia Order Book, 1787, Part 2

Caroline County, Virginia Order Book, 1787–1788

Caroline County, Virginia Order Book, 1788

Culpeper County, Virginia Deed Book Abstracts, 1769–1773

Culpeper County, Virginia Deed Book Abstracts,1778–1779

Culpeper County, Virginia Deed Book Abstracts, 1781–1783

Culpeper County, Virginia Deed Book Abstracts, 1785–1786

Culpeper County, Virginia Deed Book Abstracts,1788–1789

Culpeper County, Virginia Deed Book Abstracts, 1791–1792

Culpeper County, Virginia Deed Book Abstracts, 1795–1796

Culpeper County, Virginia Land Tax Book, 1782 1786

Culpeper County, Virginia Land Tax Book, 1787–1789

Culpeper County, Virginia Minute Book, 1763–1764

Digest of Family Relationships, 1650–1692, from Virginia County Court Records

Digest of Family Relationships, 1720–1750, from Virginia County Court Records

Digest of Family Relationships, 1750–1763, from Virginia County Court Records

Digest of Family Relationships, 1764–1775, from Virginia County Court Records

Essex County, Virginia Deed and Will Abstracts, 1695–1697

Essex County, Virginia Deed and Will Abstracts, 1697–1699

Essex County, Virginia Deed and Will Abstracts, 1699–1701

Essex County, Virginia Deed and Will Abstracts, 1701–1703

Essex County, Virginia Deed and Will Abstracts, 1745–1749

Essex County, Virginia Deed and Will Book, 1692–1693

Essex County, Virginia Deed and Will Book, 1693–1694

Essex County, Virginia Deed and Will Book, 1694–1695

Essex County, Virginia Deed and Will Book, 1701–1704

Essex County, Virginia Deed, 1753–1754 and Will Book 1750

Essex County, Virginia Deed Abstracts, 1721–1724

Essex County, Virginia Deed Book, 1724–1728

Essex County, Virginia Deed Book, 1728–1733

Essex County, Virginia Deed Book, 1733–1738

Essex County, Virginia Deed Book, 1738–1742

Essex County, Virginia Deed Book, 1742–1745

Essex County, Virginia Deed Book, 1749–1751

Essex County, Virginia Deed Book, 1751–1753

Essex County, Virginia Land Trials Abstracts, 1711–1716 and 1715–1741

Essex County, Virginia Order Book Abstracts, 1695–1699

Essex County, Virginia Order Book Abstracts, 1699–1702

Essex County, Virginia Order Book Abstracts, 1716–1723, Part 1

Essex County, Virginia Order Book Abstracts, 1716–1723, Part 2

Essex County, Virginia Order Book Abstracts, 1716–1723, Part 3

Essex County, Virginia Order Book Abstracts, 1716–1723, Part 4

Essex County, Virginia Order Book Abstracts, 1723–1725, Part 1

Essex County, Virginia Order Book Abstracts, 1723–1725, Part 2

Essex County, Virginia Order Book Abstracts, 1725–1729, Part 1

Essex County, Virginia Order Book Abstracts, 1727–1729

Essex County, Virginia Order Book, 1695–1699

Essex County, Virginia Will Abstracts, 1730–1735

Essex County, Virginia Will Abstracts, 1735–1743

Essex County, Virginia Will Abstracts, 1745–1748

Fairfax County, Virginia Deed Abstracts, 1799–1800 and 1803–1804

Fairfax County, Virginia Deed Abstracts, 1804–1805

Fairfax County, Virginia Deed Book Abstracts, 1799

Fairfax County, Virginia Deed Book, 1798–1799

Fairfax County, Virginia Land Causes, 1788–1824

Fauquier County, Virginia Minute Book Abstracts, 1759–1761

Fauquier County, Virginia Minute Book Abstracts, 1761–1762

Fauquier County, Virginia Minute Book Abstracts, 1762–1763

Fauquier County, Virginia Minute Book Abstracts, 1763–1764

Fauquier County, Virginia Minute Book Abstracts, 1764–1766

Fauquier County, Virginia Minute Book Abstracts, 1766–1767

Fauquier County, Virginia Minute Book Abstracts, 1767–1769

Fauquier County, Virginia Minute Book Abstracts, 1769–1771

Fredericksburg City, Virginia Deed Book, 1782–1787

Fredericksburg City, Virginia Deed Book, 1787–1794

Fredericksburg City, Virginia Deed Book, 1794–1804

Hanover County, Virginia Land Tax Book, 1782–1788

Hanover County, Virginia Land Tax Book, 1789–1793

Hanover County, Virginia Land Tax Book, 1793–1796

King George County, Virginia Order Book Abstracts, 1721–1723

King George County, Virginia Deed Book Abstracts, 1721–1735

King George County, Virginia Deed Book Abstracts, 1735–1752

King George County, Virginia Deed Book Abstracts, 1753–1773

King George County, Virginia Deed Book Abstracts, 1773–1783

King George County, Virginia Will Book Abstracts, 1752–1780

King William County, Virginia Record Book, 1702–1705

King William County, Virginia Record Book, 1705–1721

King William County, Virginia Record Book, 1722
and 1785–1786

Lancaster County, Virginia Deed and Will Book, 1652–1657

Lancaster County, Virginia Deed and Will Book, 1654–1661

Lancaster County, Virginia Deed and Will Book, 1661–1702
(1661–1666 and 1699–1702)

Lancaster County, Virginia Deed Book Abstracts, 1701–1706

Lancaster County, Virginia Deed Book, 1710–1714

Lancaster County, Virginia Order Book Abstracts, 1656–1661

Lancaster County, Virginia Order Book Abstracts, 1662–1666

Lancaster County, Virginia Order Book Abstracts, 1666–1669

Lancaster County, Virginia Order Book Abstracts, 1670–1674

Lancaster County, Virginia Order Book Abstracts, 1674–1678

Lancaster County, Virginia Order Book Abstracts, 1678–1681

Lancaster County, Virginia Order Book Abstracts, 1682–1687

Lancaster County, Virginia Order Book Abstracts, 1729–1732

Lancaster County, Virginia Order Book Abstracts, 1736–1739

Lancaster County, Virginia Order Book Abstracts, 1739–1742

Lancaster County, Virginia Order Book, 1687–1691

Lancaster County, Virginia Order Book, 1691–1695

Lancaster County, Virginia Order Book, 1695–1699

Lancaster County, Virginia Order Book, 1699–1701

Lancaster County, Virginia Order Book, 1701–1703

Lancaster County, Virginia Order Book, 1703–1706

Lancaster County, Virginia Order Book, 1732–1736

Lancaster County, Virginia Will Book, 1675–1689

Loudoun County, Virginia Order Book, 1763–1764

Loudoun County, Virginia Order Book, 1764

Louisa County, Virginia Deed Book, 1744–1746

Louisa County, Virginia Order Book, 1742–1744

Madison County, Virginia Deed Book Abstracts, 1793–1804

Madison County, Virginia Deed Book, 1793–1813,
and Marriage Bonds, 1793–1800

Middlesex County, Virginia Deed Book, 1679–1688

Middlesex County, Virginia Deed Book, 1688–1694

Middlesex County, Virginia Deed Book, 1694–1703

Middlesex County, Virginia Deed Book, 1703–1709

Middlesex County, Virginia Deed Book, 1709–1720

Middlesex County, Virginia Order Book Abstracts, 1686–1690

Middlesex County, Virginia Order Book Abstracts, 1697–1700

Middlesex County, Virginia Record Book, 1721–1813

Northumberland County, Virginia Deed and Will Book, 1650–1655

Northumberland County, Virginia Deed and Will Book, 1655–1658

Northumberland County, Virginia Deed and Will Book, 1658–1662

Northumberland County, Virginia Deed and Will Book, 1662–1666

Northumberland County, Virginia Deed and Will Book, 1666–1670

Northumberland County, Virginia Deed and Will Book, 1670–1672
and 1706–1711

Northumberland County, Virginia Deed and Will Book, 1711–1712

Northumberland County, Virginia Order Book, 1652–1657

Northumberland County, Virginia Order Book, 1657–1661

Northumberland County, Virginia Order Book, 1665–1669

Northumberland County, Virginia Order Book, 1669–1673

Northumberland County, Virginia Order Book, 1680–1683

Northumberland County, Virginia Order Book, 1683–1686

Northumberland County, Virginia Order Book, 1699–1700

Northumberland County, Virginia Order Book, 1700–1702

Northumberland County, Virginia Order Book, 1702–1704

Orange County, Virginia, Chancery Suits, 1831–1845

Orange County, Virginia Deeds, 1743–1759

Orange County, Virginia Deed Book Abstracts, 1759–1778

Orange County, Virginia Deed Book Abstracts, 1778–1786

Orange County, Virginia Deed Book Abstracts, 1795–1797

Orange County, Virginia Deed Book Abstracts, 1797–1799

Orange County, Virginia Deed Book Abstracts, 1799–1800

Orange County, Virginia Deed Book Abstracts, 1800–1802

Orange County, Virginia Deed Book Abstracts, 1786–1791,
Deed Book 19

Orange County, Virginia Deed Book Abstracts, 1791–1795,
Deed Book 20

Orange County, Virginia Land Tax Book, 1782–1790

Orange County, Virginia Land Tax Book, 1791–1795

Orange County, Virginia Order Book Abstracts, 1747–1748

Orange County, Virginia Order Book Abstracts, 1748–1749

Orange County, Virginia Order Book Abstracts, 1749–1752

Orange County, Virginia Order Book Abstracts, 1752–1753

Orange County, Virginia Order Book Abstracts, 1753–1754

Orange County, Virginia Order Book Abstracts, 1755–1756

Orange County, Virginia Order Book Abstracts, 1756–1757

Orange County, Virginia Order Book Abstracts, 1757–1759

Orange County, Virginia Order Book Abstracts, 1759–1762

Orange County, Virginia Order Book Abstracts, 1762–1763

Orange County, Virginia Will Abstracts, 1778–1821

Orange County, Virginia Will Abstracts, 1821–1838

Orange County, Virginia, Will Digest, 1734–1838

Pamunkey Neighbors of Orange County, Virginia (Transcriptions from the original files of County Courts in Virginia, Kentucky and Missouri of wills, deeds, order books & marriages as well as some family lines...)

A Supplement to Pamunkey Neighbors of Orange County, Virginia, Volumes 1 and 2

Ruth and Sam Sparacio, Luretta and Eldon Corkill

Petersburg City, Virginia Hustings Court Deed Book Abstracts, 1784–1787

Petersburg City, Virginia Hustings Court Deed Book Abstracts, 1787–1790

Petersburg City, Virginia Hustings Court Deed Book Abstracts, 1790–1793

Prince William County, Virginia Deed Book Abstracts, 1749–1752

Prince William County, Virginia Order Book Abstracts, 1752–1753

Prince William County, Virginia Order Book Abstracts, 1753–1757

(Old) Rappahannock County, Virginia Deed and Will Book Abstracts, 1656–1662

(Old) Rappahannock County, Virginia Deed and Will Book Abstracts, 1662–1665

(Old) Rappahannock County, Virginia Deed and Will Book Abstracts, 1663–1668

(Old) Rappahannock County, Virginia Deed and Will Book Abstracts, 1665–1677

(Old) Rappahannock County, Virginia Deed and Will Book Abstracts, 1668–1670

(Old) Rappahannock County, Virginia Deed and Will Book Abstracts, 1670–1672

(Old) Rappahannock County, Virginia Deed and Will Book Abstracts, 1672–1673/4

(Old) Rappahannock County, Virginia Deed and Will Book Abstracts, 1673/4–1676

(Old) Rappahannock County, Virginia Deed and Will Book Abstracts, 1677–1678/9

(Old) Rappahannock County, Virginia Deed and Will Book Abstracts, 1678/9–1682

(Old) Rappahannock County, Virginia Deed and Will Book Abstracts, 1682–1686

(Old) Rappahannock County, Virginia Deed and Will Book Abstracts, 1686–1688

(Old) Rappahannock County, Virginia Deed and Will Book Abstracts, 1688–1692

(Old) Rappahannock County, Virginia Order Book Abstracts, 1683–1685

(Old) Rappahannock County, Virginia Order Book Abstracts, 1689–1692

(Old) Rappahannock County, Virginia Will Book Abstracts, 1682–1687

Richmond County, Virginia Deed Book Abstracts, 1692–1695

Richmond County, Virginia Deed Book Abstracts, 1695–1701

Richmond County, Virginia Deed Book Abstracts, 1701–1704

Richmond County, Virginia Deed Book Abstracts, 1705–1708

Richmond County, Virginia Deed Book Abstracts, 1708–1711

Richmond County, Virginia Deed Book Abstracts, 1711–1714

Richmond County, Virginia Deed Book Abstracts, 1715–1718

Richmond County, Virginia Deed Book Abstracts, 1718–1719

Richmond County, Virginia Deed Book Abstracts, 1719–1721

Richmond County, Virginia Deed Book Abstracts, 1721–1725

Richmond County, Virginia Order Book Abstracts, 1694–1697

Richmond County, Virginia Order Book Abstracts, 1697–1699

Richmond County, Virginia Order Book Abstracts, 1699–1701

Richmond County, Virginia Order Book Abstracts, 1714–1715

Richmond County, Virginia Order Book Abstracts, 1719–1721

Richmond County, Virginia Order Book Abstracts, 1721–1725

Richmond County, Virginia Order Book, 1692–1694

Richmond County, Virginia Order Book, 1702–1704

Richmond County, Virginia Order Book, 1717–1718

Richmond County, Virginia Order Book, 1718–1719

Spotsylvania County, Virginia Deed Book, 1722–1725

Spotsylvania County, Virginia Deed Book, 1725–1728

Spotsylvania County, Virginia Deed Book: 1730–1731

Spotsylvania County, Virginia Order Book Abstracts, 1742–1744

Spotsylvania County, Virginia Order Book Abstracts, 1744–1746

Stafford County, Virginia Deed and Will Book, 1686–1689

Stafford County, Virginia Deed and Will Book, 1689–1693

Stafford County, Virginia Deed and Will Book, 1699–1709

Stafford County, Virginia Deed and Will Book, 1780–1786, and Scheme Book Orders, 1790–1793

Stafford County, Virginia Deed Book, 1722–1728 and 1755–1765

Stafford County, Virginia Order Book, 1664–1668 and 1689–1690

Stafford County, Virginia Order Book, 1691–1692

Stafford County, Virginia Order Book, 1692–1693

Stafford County, Virginia Will Book, 1729–1748

Stafford County, Virginia Will Book, 1748–1767

Westmoreland County, Virginia Deed and Will Abstracts, 1723–1726

Westmoreland County, Virginia Deed and Will Abstracts, 1726–1729

Westmoreland County, Virginia Deed and Will Abstracts, 1729–1732

Westmoreland County, Virginia Deed and Will Abstracts, 1732–1734

Westmoreland County, Virginia Deed and Will Abstracts, 1734–1736

Westmoreland County, Virginia Deed and Will Abstracts, 1736–1740

Westmoreland County, Virginia Deed and Will Abstracts, 1740–1742

Westmoreland County, Virginia Deed and Will Abstracts, 1742–1745

Westmoreland County, Virginia Deed and Will Abstracts, 1745–1747

Westmoreland County, Virginia Deed and Will Abstracts, 1747–1748

Westmoreland County, Virginia Deed and Will Abstracts, 1749–1751

Westmoreland County, Virginia Deed and Will Abstracts, 1751–1754

Westmoreland County, Virginia Deed and Will Abstracts, 1754–1756

Westmoreland County, Virginia Order Book, 1705–1707

Westmoreland County, Virginia Order Book, 1707–1709

Westmoreland County, Virginia Order Book, 1709–1712